Plant Based D For Bodybuilding

The Plant-Based And High-Protein Guide To Increase Muscle Mass With Healthy And Whole-Food Vegan Recipes To Fuel Your Workouts

Michael Gill

Table of Contents

Introduction

What Entails A Plant-Based Diet

The plant is a good source of closely all the nutrients required by the human body. Plant based diets include fruits, vegetables, nuts, whole grain, and legumes. These are basically plant based foods and hole foods. With the realization of the various health benefits attributed to plant proteins, people have shifted from consuming animal foods to plant-based foods. Plant based diet includes all unprocessed plant foods. It excludes the consumption of processed foods such as pasta and sugars. It excludes processed fruit juices, milk and milk products, all forms of meat (white and red), and eggs.

Foods To Keep Off When On A Plant-Based Diet Are As Follows

Avoid eating processed foods such as pasta and canned foods. Instead, go for fresh and whole foods. Processed foods are low in their fiber content; they also have other additives such as sugar, salt, preservatives, excess oils, and fats. These foods are linked to the development of chronic illnesses such as cancer, diabetes, hypertension, kidney disease, and heart problems, among others. These foods are also a significant contributor to obesity and weight challenges.

Plant based diet excludes all animal products such as eggs, milk products, poultry, red meat, fish, and any other foods obtained from animals. Animal products are linked to the development of cancers in the human body, especially the heme iron contained in red meat. When animal products are cooked up to certain temperatures, they emit carcinogenic compounds that lead to development of cancer cells. These foods are also a major contributor to weight gain. Research has shown that it is rather a difficulty to watch weight while still on animal products. Animal related foods are also high in their fat contents and have zero fiber. Consumption of animal products leads to heart problems and hypertension as a result of clogged blood vessels. Their low fiber content makes it a cause of stomach problems such as indigestion and diarrhea.

Avoid the consumption of fast foods such as fries, burgers, cakes, ice cream, and pizza, among others. Fast foods have contents such as processed sugars and high sodium content, high fat content. These foods induce cravings in your body that lead to excessive eating and obesity. The foods are also very unhealthy as they contribute to increased risk of chronic illnesses such as cancer, hypertension, diabetes, heart problems, among others. Fast foods are also low in their nutrient content. Being addictive, when a person forms a habit of consuming fast foods, their bodies go low on some essential nutrients such as vitamins and minerals. They also contain additives that you do not want to put in your bodies due to their toxic nature.

Health Benefits Of Plant Diets

Plant foods offer a wide range of advantages over animal foods. They are scientifically recommended for healthy living as they promote a person's wellbeing. By eating plant-based foods, a person is able to reduce the risk of certain illnesses and avoid problems associated with overweight/obesity.

Plant foods are advantageous in their low fat and calorie load. They are also dense in their protein content. Proteins are excellent in helping a person watch weight as they prevent the gaining of body fat. By consuming plant proteins, a person produces more weight limiting hormones. Proteins also help in weight reduction by reducing the feelings of hunger while at the same time increasing the metabolic rate of the body.

By consuming plant products, a person reduces the risk of being overweight. Plants offer excellent sources of fiber, antioxidants, minerals, and vitamins. Plant foods are mainly high in fiber which is helpful in digestion as it limits the amount of sugars absorbed in the digestion process. The fiber in plant foods is also helpful in reducing cholesterol by preventing the absorption of fats in the foods we take. Fiber also helps in preventing constipation in enhancing the digestion of foods. It helps in the stimulation of the various digestive organs to produce important digestive juices. Enough intake of dietary fiber prolongs the amount of time food takes to move through the canal, increasing the absorption of minerals and vitamins in the food. It also prevents diarrhea and excessive hardening of stool.

Research has also confirmed that people who take foods high in fiber are at a lower risk of gaining weight. By consuming foods high in fiber, a person reduces the chances of developing type 2 diabetes. The reason behind the fiber preventing the occurrence of type 2 diabetes is the ability of the fiber to reduce the amounts of sugar the body absorbs maintaining a healthy blood sugar level.

It is also attributed to lowered cholesterol and reduced risk of developing heart disease. The fiber in the digestive system also clumps fats reducing the rate at which they are digested and absorbed in the body. Healthy bacteria in the gut thrive on soluble fiber. The bacteria microbiome feeds on the remains of fermented fiber in the digestive system. These bacteria help in the production of short-chain fatty-acids that help in reducing cholesterol in the body. The short chain fatty-acids also promote good health by reducing inflammation in the body. Inflammation is a risky condition linked to the development of serious illnesses such as cancer among others.

Plant foods reduce the risk of cancers, such as colorectal cancer. While animal foods are found to increase the risk of cancer, plants contain phytochemicals and antioxidants that reduce the risk of developing cancer while at the same time fighting the progress of cancer cells. The fiber found in plant foods is also helpful in detoxification of the body. The detoxification process is aided by both soluble and insoluble fiber. The soluble fiber absorbs the excess hormones and toxins within the body, preventing them from being taken up by the cells. Insoluble fiber works by preventing the absorptions of toxins fond in the foods we consume from the digestive track. It also increases the time which food takes to go through the digestive track. The process is said to reduce the body's demands for more food. The soluble fiber also stimulates the production of certain components that reduce the feelings of hunger which include peptide YY, peptide-1, and cholecystokinin.

When a person is on a plant-based diet, they cut on their consumption of processed foods and refined sugars that are harmful to the body. These sugars promote weight gain by increased food cravings and the production of certain hormones that induce the body to crave for food. These sugars and other additives found in processed food also increase the risk of cancer and among other illnesses.

Plant foods are also rich in certain components that are found to possess anti-oxidation properties while also working in reducing cholesterol levels in the body. These components are polyphenols, such as flavonoids, stilbenoids, and lignans. For instance, green tea, which is most commonly used for its anti-oxidation properties is rich in (epigallocatechin gallate) a flavonoid responsible for the production of the fat burning hormone.

Another beauty of eating plant foods is that you worry less about overeating. The plant foods contain limited calories and negligible levels of harmful fats. According to research, persons who eat plant foods live longer as compared to those that feed on animal foods. Plants foods not only improve the quality of life by protecting a person from illnesses but also lower the risk of early deaths resulting from these illnesses and health conditions.

Plant based foods are also friendly to the environment. Eating plant foods encourages the planting of more plants to give more foods that protect the ozone layer by absorbing excess harmful carbon dioxide from the atmosphere. Plants based diet discourages the industrial practices associated with processing foods. These practices promote the release of harmful gases into the atmosphere, and the packaging of the foods makes use of materials that are not environmentally friendly.

Plant Based Bodybuilding: Getting Started

Plant Based Diet

On the other hand, this type of diet shares a similarity with veganism in the sense that it also does not promote dietary consumption of animal-based products. This includes dairy, meat, and eggs. The idea here is to make a diet out of minimally processed to unprocessed fruits, veggies, whole grains, nuts, seeds, and legumes. So, there will be NO Oreo cookies for you.

Whole-food plant-based diet followers are often driven by the health benefits it brings. It is a diet that has very little to do with restricting calories or counting macros but mostly to do with preventing and reversing illnesses.

How To Get Started On A Plant-Based Diet

A common misconception among many people – even some of those in the health and fitness industry is that anyone who switches to a plant-based diet automatically becomes super healthy. There are tons of plant-based junk foods out there which can really derail your health goals if you are constantly consuming them. Committing to healthy foods is the only way that you can achieve health benefits. On the other hand, these plant-based snacks do play a role in keeping you motivated. They should be consumed in moderation, sparingly and in small bits. As you will come to see later on in this book, there is a topic dedicated to giving ideas on plant-based snacks you can whip up at home. So, without further ado, this is how you get started on a whole food plant-based recipe.

Decide What a Plant-Based Diet Means for You Making a decision to structure how your plant-based diet is going to look is the first step, and it is going to help you transition from your current diet outlook. This is something that is really personal and varies from one person to the other. While some people decide that they will not tolerate any animal products at all, some make do with tiny bits of dairy or meat occasionally. It is really up to you to decide what and how you want your plant-based diet to look like. The most important thing is that whole plant-based foods have to make a great majority of your diet.

Understand What You Are Eating All right, now that you've gotten the decision part down, your next task is going to involve a lot of analysis on your part. What do we mean by this? Well, if this is your first time trying out the plant-based diet, you may be surprised by the number of foods, especially packaged foods, which contain animal products. You will find yourself nurturing the habit of reading labels while you are shopping.

Find Revamped Versions of Your Favorite Recipes I'm sure you have a number of favorite dishes that are not necessarily plant based. For most people, leaving all that behind is usually the hardest part. However, there is still a way you could meet halfway. Take some time to ponder what you like about those non-plant-based meals. Think along the lines of flavor, texture, versatility and so on; and look for swaps in the whole food plant-based diet that can fulfill what you will be missing. Just to give you some insight into what I mean, here are a couple of examples: Crumbled or blended tofu would make for a decent filling in both sweet and savory dishes just like ricotta cheese would in lasagna. Lentils go particularly well with saucy dishes that are typically associated with meatloaf and Bolognese.

As you read on, you will come across dedicated to an assortment of delectable main course recipes that are purely plant-based. All in all, when this is executed right, you will not even miss your non-plant based favorite meals.

Build A Support Network

Building any new habit is tough, but it doesn't have to be. Find yourself some friends, or even relatives, who are willing to lead this lifestyle with you. This will help you stay focused and motivated while also providing emotional support and some form of accountability. You can do fun stuff like trying out and sharing new recipes with these friends or even hitting up restaurants that offer a variety of plant-based options. You can even go a step further and look up local plant-based groups on social media to help you expand your knowledge and support network.

The Incredible Health Benefits

More and more people are becoming aware of this diet as a channel to enhance weight loss, alleviate and even cure many chronic diseases. So, let's check out some of the health benefits of following a plant-based plan.

It Lowers Blood Pressure

Plant-based foods tend to have a higher amount of potassium whose benefits, notably include reducing blood pressure and alleviating stress and anxiety. Some foods rich in potassium include legumes, nuts, seeds, whole grains, and fruits. Meat, on the other hand, contains very little to no potassium.

It Lowers Cholesterol

Plants do not contain any traces of cholesterol. Leading a plant-based lifestyle will, therefore, help you lower the levels of cholesterol in your body leading to reduced risks of heart disease.

Checks Your Blood Sugar Levels

Plant-based foods tend to have a lot of fiber. This helps slow down the absorption of sugars into the bloodstream as well as keep you feeling full for longer periods of time. It also helps balance out your blood cortisol levels thereby reducing stress.

It Helps Prevent and Fight Off Chronic Diseases

In societies where a majority of people lead a plant-based lifestyle the rates of chronic diseases such as cancer, obesity, and diabetes are usually very low. This diet has also been proven to lengthen the lives of those already suffering from these chronic diseases.

It Is Good for Weight Loss

Consuming whole plant-based foods make it easier to cut off excess weight and maintain a healthier weight without having to involve calorie restrictions. You can lose weight naturally by taking more vitamins, fiber, and minerals than you do animal fats and proteins.

More Energy And Efficiency

The food groups that are part of the plant-based diet are rich in good fats and nutrients that provide instant energy to the body and cutting down the meat; you can reap a lot of health benefits.

Lower The Rate Of Cancer And Cardiovascular Diseases.

The good fat and omega 3 rich food help lower the fat. The whole foods plant-based diet improves the chances of avoiding cancer as we cut on red meat, smoking, and alcohol, and we all know all these items are a link to increased heart diseases.

What Some Influential People Think Of A Plant-Based Lifestyle

Whether we like to admit it or not, celebrities do have a lot of influence, which can either be exercised in promoting good or promoting evil. We have already explored some of the numerous benefits of going plant based. Some celebrities are passively plant-based diet followers; this means that their fame and power is not a result of the diets they follow, but because of something different like their roles in the respective industries. Others are active plant-based diet followers whose claim to fame is putting in some added value and quality to the talks and discussions on the plant-based diet and lifestyle.

What To Look Out For When Adopting This Lifestyle

For most people looking to go plant-based, protein is always a major concern. There is this notion that's perpetuated by the mainstream media backed by big meat producers that protein is only found in meat. Well, that's just not true. Traditional staples such as nuts, beans, oats and brown rice come with a lot of protein.

Often times, nutrients like calcium are also said to come from only animal-based sources. The truth is that foods like kale, broccoli, and almonds contain lots of calcium. Ask yourself this, if calcium comes from meat, then where did the animal get it from? It's definitely from the greens they eat.

The major concern for most plant-based diet followers is usually vitamin B12. This great vitamin is mostly found in cereals and plant-based milk (fortified products). However, you should not rely on these products to get enough vitamin B12. The best option is to take vitamin b12 supplements (sublingual); just to make sure that there are no issues.

You can adopt a healthy plant-based lifestyle by basing your diet around cooked and raw foods filled with leafy and colorful veggies. These will provide your body with the nutrients and requirements it needs.

Plant-Based Protein Sources

The following are the known sources of proteins, and they should be added to a vegan diet to make it rich in proteins.

• Beans and legumes: These are an excellent source of protein. There are lots of fibers present in legumes and beans. However, they are also rich in carbs, so their intake should be limited in a day or per serving.

• Hemp, flax, sunflower, and chia seeds: Seeds are a great source of protein and omega 3s. Where vegans can't have seafood and meat, they can meet their protein needs with plant-based seeds. They are also full of essential oils.

• Quinoa and amaranth: They are also known as the pseudo-grains because they are low-carb grains and serve as the best option for bodybuilders. They are full of proteins and make up a healthy breakfast.

• Meat substitutes: There are several peas and soy-based products which can be used as a substitute for meat like tempeh, or tofu, etc. Edamame, soy protein powder, and soymilk are other good sources of protein.

• Plant-based milk and yogurts: Coconut milk, coconut cream, yogurt, etc.

• Spirulina: A blue-green algae which is full of proteins, vitamins, and minerals. It is great to add to smoothies and shakes.

• There are several vegan protein powders that can be used in snacks, desserts, and energy bars.

• Nutritional yeast: It is most often used in doughs and baked goods; the yeast is mixed with vitamin B12 during production, and it is also a good source of protein.

• Sprouted grain bread: These breads not only provide us with protein, but they are also a good source of complex carbohydrates.

• Oats: Often used in oatmeal, the oats are rich in protein, and they are full of fibers. Overnight oatmeal and oats porridges with fruits are a good option for a vegan diet.

• Fruit and vegetables: Though not all vegetables and fruits contain high doses of protein, they sure complement the vegan diet well by providing lots of fiber and calories.

• Whole grains and cereals: All grains and cereal are proven to be a good source of fibers, vitamin B, and protein.

- Nuts and nut butter: Nuts are good for a vegan diet due to their rich protein content, and nut butter is a perfect substitute for animal-based butter or fats. Peanut butter and almond butter can be used in this regard.

- Tahini: It is a thick paste made out of sesame seeds, and like its source, it is also full of protein and essential oils.

- Healthy oils: All plant-based oil is considered healthy for a vegan diet. There are some plant oils that are rich in omega 3s like avocado oil, hempseeds, and olive oil.

- Vegan dark chocolate: Dark chocolate is a good source of antioxidants and has all the necessary micronutrients which are essential for a vegan diet like vitamins A, B, E, magnesium, iron, potassium, and calcium.

Food to Avoid on a Plant-Based Diet

It is important to have a quick overview of the things that should be avoided:

- Eggs, dairy, meat, fish, poultry, and products produced by bees are strictly restricted on the plant-based diet. Similarly, food that contains any part of those items or that are extracted from them is also forbidden. Animal-based preservatives should also be avoided.

- There are some other ingredients that may be vegan in composition but for a vegan diet that is used for physical fitness, items like deep-fried foods, fast foods, candy, fried chips, etc., should be avoided.

- Junk food, whether it is vegan or not, is always unhealthy and should be looked out for. Things like ice cream or protein bars that say they are vegan should still be avoided because of the high dose of refined carbs they carry.

Macronutrients

Macronutrients are responsible for providing energy and basic building blocks to the body. Lack of these nutrients directly causes malnutrition and all the related health problems. They are required in large amounts for body growth and daily functioning. The sources of macronutrients in a plant-based diet are as follows:

1.   Protein sources

Protein is most important to look for on a plant-based bodybuilding diet. You can find a good amount of protein in the following food items:

- Tempeh
- Tofu
- Seitan
- Edamame
- Lentils
- Chickpeas
- Nutritional yeast
- Quinoa
- Hempseed
- Peas
- Amaranth
- Tiff
- Oats

2.   Carb sources

Carbohydrates are essential for metabolic activities, but their intake should be controlled to avoid a glucose spike in the blood and to prevent insulin resistance. Complex carbohydrates are considered healthier than refined carbs like those present in sugar. On a plant-based vegan diet, the following are good options for carb intake:

- Black/brown rice
- Sweet potatoes
- Quinoa
- Lentils
- Oats
- Limited amount of bread and pasta.

3.   Fat sources

Plants are an excellent source of healthy unsaturated fats, and you can use them from the following sources for a vegan diet:

- Avocado
- Flax seeds
- Chia seeds
- Almonds
- Almond butter
- Brazil nuts
- Walnuts
- Pumpkin seeds
- Cashew nuts
- Coconut

Micronutrient Intake

Nutrients that are required in small and trace amounts by the body but yet are vital for metabolic activities. They are the catalyst to many of the enzymic cavities and their deficiency can lead to serious health problems. Being on a vegan diet does restrict a person from getting a healthy number of micronutrients; there are many plant-based options for these nutrients, as follows:

1.   Vitamin B12

Vitamin B12 is largely found in plants that are grown in a B12-rich soil. Organic products like mushrooms, nutritional yeast, noir, and spirulina are all full of B12. The deficiency of B12 can hamper the normal production of red blood cells. This can deprive the muscles of much-needed energy and oxygen. Most of the soil-grown vegetables lose their B12 when washed or cooked. The best way to maintain the healthy intake of B12 is to use products that are fortified with B12 such as plant milk, cereals, soy products, and yeast.

2. Vitamin D

This fat-soluble vitamin plays a major role in the absorption of calcium and phosphorus. Vitamin D deficiency can also lead to bone weakness despite normal calcium intake. A small amount of vitamin D is present in plant-based food but mostly can be sourced directly from the sunlight. People who don't go out much in the sunlight suffer from its deficiency. Sitting for just 15 minutes in the sun is important to absorb vitamin D.

3. Long-chain omega-3s

Omega fatty acids are largely present in seafood, so it is assumed that a plant-based diet can deprive us of the much-needed omega 3 and omega 6, but that is not true. There are certain algae oils, sunflower seeds, hemp seeds, and other seeds that are rich in omega 3 fatty acids—whereas the need for omega 6 fatty acids can be met with the use of sunflower oil, sesame oils, safflower, and corn oils.

4. Iodine

For a normal thyroid function, iodine is essential to consume. The thyroid is responsible for controlling our metabolic rate, and the inefficiency of the thyroid leads to poor metabolic activity. Iodine is not largely present in the food we eat, but it is added to salt to produce iodized salt. This salt can maintain the level of iodine in the blood.

5. Iron

Iron is vital to red blood cells and to the formation of new DNA. It is capable of carrying oxygen and aids in energy metabolism. Its deficiency can, therefore, lead to several health problems. Vegans should focus on their iron intake and look for the ingredients which are rich in iron like seeds, nuts, dry fruits, beans, vegetables, and peas. There are special iron-fortified products in the market like iron-fortified bread, cereals, plant milk, etc., which should be added to the diet.

6. Calcium

Calcium is the mineral that supports bone growth and repair which is important to sustain muscle growth, especially when a person is weight lifting. It is also essential for muscle function, cardiac function, and nerve impulse. Lack of calcium can sometimes cause muscle stiffness, spasms, or weakness. Plant-based food that is rich in calcium mainly includes turnip greens, watercress, chickpeas, broccoli, calcium tofu, kale, bok choy, and calcium-fortified juice and milk.

The average calcium intake should not be less than 525 mg per day. Calcium supplements can also be used to meet an individual's needs.

7.   Zinc

Zinc is another mineral that is vital for better immunity, metabolism, and cell repair. Vegans can maximize their zinc intake by consuming more whole grains, seeds, nuts, legumes, tofu, and wheat germ. Fermented foods such as miso, sauerkraut, and tempeh are also good for zinc intake. Soak legumes, seeds, and nuts in water overnight and then eat them to increase the absorption of zinc in the body.

Eliminate Weight With Protein Diet

It is a natural fact that only through watching what we eat, will we have the most impact on our weight. This is where the plant-based diet really shines and lets you enjoy automatic, effortless fat burning without all the usual calorie constraints of other diets.

Weight loss is an almost certain result you will enjoy once you start the plant-based diet, but this is not the only benefit that you will enjoy. Think of all those activities you have always wanted to pursue but shelved because you simply had no energy left after your usual day's work.

Well, time to dust off those hobbies and the things you enjoy doing, because on the plant-based, you will have more energy for your daily work and play! The accompanying mental clarity and sharpness of thought are also positive effects which you will have as a direct result of the diet. A better health report card, by way of optimized cholesterol readings, normalized blood sugar and a corresponding lowered risk of cardiovascular diseases are also just some of the beneficial health effects experienced by most on the diet.

The benefits of a particular diet may be numerous, but if you are forced to have the same stuff every breakfast, lunch and dinner, even the most avid supporter of the lot would probably have problems sustaining the diet. This is where I am most happy to say that the plant-based diet has quite some leeway for the concoction of various different recipes, and it is the purpose of this book to bring you some of the more delicious and easy-to-prepare meals for your gastronomic pleasure!

For the beginners as well as the adepts, the recipes contained within are created specifically to be appealing to your palate while not requiring you to literally spend the whole day in the kitchen! Concise and to the point, the recipes break down meal preparation requirements in a simple step by step format, easy for anyone to understand. An additional 21-day meal plan is also structured to serve both as guidance as well as inspiration for the new and old adherents to the diet.

Don't Forget To Exercise

It has always been said that dieting is an effective way to lose weight. However, to keep the weight off, exercise is required. Many studies have shown that exercising while dieting is actually the best way to lose weight. Firstly, the diet becomes more effective and you lose weight faster if you exercise. But it also gets you in the habit of continuing your exercise when your diet is complete.

The exercise expected is not something that is not achievable either. Even with just forty-five minutes of exercise each day, can increase your weight loss by over ten percent! Anything that can get your heartbeat pulsing higher and faster than normal is considered exercise.

Often times, dieting will make you lose weight in many parts that you don't want to lose weight in, such as curvaceous or softening lines. Studies have shown that combined with exercise, dieting can help reduce your body mass index, waist circumference, and percentage of body fat.

Another concern is that with dieting, often times you appear lighter because your muscle and bone density is reduced. That is not a healthy lifestyle in the long term. Exercising will stimulate the growth of your muscles and have your body burn the fat instead of your metabolic tissues.

It is also important to understand that the idea behind dieting is that most people want to look skinnier and overall better. However, lean is what will make you look perfect! Being lean will highlight your figure and keep your body healthy and toned. Skinny means that you have lost a lot of muscle density and water retention. In the long run, it can affect your calcium, iron, and zinc levels in your body.

Kick-Starting Your Weight-Loss Journey

To get things done the right way and to ensure your body benefits from this diet, it is essential to consider the following things prior to starting this regimen.

Well Organized Meal plan

Please note that the main purpose of this book and diet plan is to help you lose weight and help in maintaining a healthy lifestyle. Because of this, you have to follow a strict plan to achieve your goals. This book provides a 21-day plant-based plan to kick-start your wellness journey. Please remember that this meal plan will require some commitment, and it is not how your diet will always be structured after the 21-day plan. After 21 days, once your body has adjusted, you will be able to make a consistent meal plan schedule where fasting is not required.

Understand Your Body

Getting your blood tested for the existence of any underlying condition is important to ensure that you start the regimen without worrying about it affecting your health negatively. Though, it doesn't harm your body, but in case you are suffering from a serious condition, it is best that you don't go on any sort of weight loss diet.

It is important to get your blood tested for lipid panel, liver and kidney function, inflammatory markers, thyroid panel and blood count.

Get enough sleep and relax efficiently

It is important that you understand that you must take this diet easy and relax while practicing it. Your goal must not be to quickly cut down your carb intake, so you can lose an enormous amount of your body weight as soon as possible. Rather, you should reduce it slowly and gradually. Don't worry; you will still benefit a lot from this plan. Going easy on yourself helps you experience less side effects and enables your body to adjust comfortably to the completely new diet plan.

Get Professional Support

It is wise to get the assistance of a professional healthcare practitioner, dietician, or nutritionist who can help you out in preparing good meal plans for you. In this case, this e-book will do this job for you by providing you with more meal plans and guidance in the next series. Nonetheless, it is a good idea to consult a professional at least once before commencing the diet just to make sure that you know your body is ready for it. You will also find it easier to prepare good meal plans that are customized just for you.

In case, you suffer from heart diseases or other conditions such as epilepsy, HBP, diabetes (TYPE 2), Alzheimer's or any other medical condition, then it is absolutely essential for you to get a professional's help before and during the plan.

Create time

This is one of the most crucial factors to consider before implementing the low-carb diet. You must not start it when you are going through an extremely hectic schedule and have no time to spare for yourself. This is because this diet demands you to prepare special meals and get used to different foods that you aren't accustomed to eating regularly. These changes will stress you out, so you need to have enough time to devote to this new routine, at least for about two weeks.

Therefore, you must start the plant-based diet when you are emotionally, psychologically, and physically relaxed and free.

Be careful with other people's opinions

If you are to achieve optimal this goal, you will definitely need to understand that you cannot just eat anything even when in social places otherwise you will end up jeopardizing your entire regime since it takes time for any carbs you take to be completely out of your body. As such, you should be psychologically prepared to take different foods that might attract some attention and well-meaning but often misleading comments about the diet. Being prepared will ensure you don't give up.

Improving Vitality and Energy

Energy and vitality are another issue people have with a plant-based diet. Even those who really want to make the switch are concerned that their energy will plummet, especially for bodybuilders. And I'll be honest, there are some plant-based dieters out there that do suffer from low energy and vitality, but that has more to do with the food they do eat than the food they don't eat. Even plant-based dieters can choose bad foods to eat that harm them more than hurt them. Did you realize Oreos and skittle are vegan? So you see, you can be vegan and eat crap that makes you feel like crap, or, you can be vegan and eat things that make you feel full of time and energetic.

But before we get looking at the foods you are eating to make sure you are gaining energy, we have to look in the obvious places. If you are feeling tired and like your day is dragging, the first thing you need to ask yourself is, "am I getting enough sleep?" Take a look at a five-year-old. Children have more energy than they can use, and they don't get it from energy drinks or coffee. All of that energy comes from the fact that they sleep upwards of ten hours each night. High energy is natural aide effect of a person who is well-rested. So the first thing you need to do is make sure you go to bed by 10 PM, or, depending on when you have to get up, make sure you get at least eight hours.

Secondly, you will want to make sure you are getting plenty of exercise. Of course, this book is geared towards bodybuilders, so that's probably not a problem. But, encase you didn't know, a sedentary life becomes a vicious cycle. When you are sedentary, your heart and muscles lose their ability to handle movement. This causes a lack of energy, which in turn causes you to stay inactive. For a person who has been mainly inactive should start by taking a brisk 30-minute walk each day, and then slowly start to up the intensity so that their heart and joints can keep up.

Thirdly, there can be a medical issue that is causing you to feel a loss of energy. If you were feeling tired before you made the switch to a plant-based diet, you might want to speak with your doctor and get tested for things like depression, thyroid problems, anemia, or other fatigue-causing diseases. Plus, vegan or not, you should probably be on a B12 supplement.

Let's move onto the food. The thing that keeps your muscles revved up is glycogen. If you placed glycogen under a powerful microscope, you would see a long, branching string of beads. All of those beads are molecules of glucose, or, simply put, sugar. Marathoners will often "carbo-load" with rice, pasta, bread, and other starchy foods before their race because as these starches are digested, they will release glucose that body has in the liver and muscles for added energy.

The majority of people would simply be excited that they were able to run a marathon. Brendan Brazier, an endurance athlete, leads the pack in the number of 50k ultramarathons and Ironman triathlons ran, and he believes deeply that food is the number one race fuel for people. He loads his diet full of healthy carbohydrates. When he was first starting his career, he found that animal products would slow his recovery time after exercising. He found that his energy returned quicker when he followed a vegan diet. Then you have Scott Jurek. Jurek ran a 100-mail Western States Endurance Run in 199. He, along with 334 other runners, took off, and Scott didn't just win the race, but he won it every year for six years in a row. He set the course record in 2004 at a time of 15 hours and 36 minutes. Much like Brendan, Scott skips meat lover's pizzas, Western omelet, and all other animal products, and sticks to a carbohydrate loaded vegan menu.

Not All Carbohydrates Are Made The Same

Carbs might be a good source of energy for vegans, but not every carb is created equal. Carbohydrates are meant for staying power. If you look at their glycemic index, you will know which ones are the best. Foods that are placed high on the glycemic index, like white potatoes, wheat, and white bread, sugar, and most cold cereals get digested too quickly and will cause a spike in your blood sugar. Then, once your blood sugar begins to return to your normal, your energy wanes, and you start having cravings.

If you pick foods that are low on the glycemic index, they treat your blood sugar nicer and will help you to avoid those highs and lows. Some of the best choices are sweet potatoes, yams, pasta, pumpernickel or rye bread, beans, and oatmeal. This isn't the only reason to avoid high glycemic foods. There's another reason as well. They will often boost your serotonin levels, which can end up causing you to feel sleepy. This doesn't happen when you choose low glycemic foods. When have that scrambled tofu or veggie bacon in the morning before your bagel, it will help to keep your energy levels from lagging.

Energy Zapping Foods

Besides high glycemic and sugary foods, you also have to watch out for extra fatty foods. You know how you feel have those huge holiday dinners around Thanksgiving, Christmas, or whatever holidays you celebrate? That's caused by all the fat in things like gravy, meats, and cheese. Animal fats and all types of saturated fat can cause your blood to become more viscous, meaning "thicker." You blood basically turns into something like oil instead of staying like water. This is probably the main reason why you end up feeling very tired after those big, heavy meals. This is also a reason why those who go vegan tend to notice their energy levels increase.

Coffee and Energy Drinks

Some people will tell you that both are bad for you and you should cut them out completely. I can't say that because I enjoy a cup of coffee each morning. As for energy drinks, I can say those are bad for you. I use to have one from time to time, but then they started to have adverse effects on me, so I stopped. Plus, they have caused heart problems for many people.

The truth is, wanting that cup of coffee each morning is due to the fact you had coffee the day before are you have to combat the withdrawals. Withdrawals from caffeine are a very real thing and can reduce your mental clarity and alertness, and will create horrible headaches. When you have that morning cup of Joe, it simply hoists you out of those withdrawals, albeit temporarily.

As for energy drinks, like Red Bull, they combine caffeine along with taurine and other additives to improve a person's alertness and athletic performance. Whether their effects are created by the caffeine or everything else in them isn't clear, but people who drink them on a regular basis experience withdrawals from them that are similar to caffeine withdrawal.

In the end, you shouldn't have to rely on caffeine to help with your energy. If you want a cup of coffee, have one. Black coffee isn't going to hurt. But you should have plenty of energy without it, so you should simply enjoy it because you like it and not because you have to have it.

Energy-Boosting Foods

I could make you spend hours looking up the glycemic index of foods, or I could simply give you my top choices for energy and vitality producing vegan-friendly foods. Which would you prefer? We're going to go over some vegan-friendly foods that will help give you energy, and you can choose how you want to enjoy them.

1.   Sweet Potatoes

These tubers are a much better alternative to the white potato. They provide loads of minerals and vitamins, such as beta-carotene, manganese, vitamin C, and disease-preventing dietary fiber. These are a great choice for bodybuilders and athletes because when they are consumed in conjunction with protein after your workout, they act as a catalyst to help the protein move into your muscle tissue and start the repairing process. Sweet potatoes are considered hypoallergenic and are one of the tops sources for post-workout carbs from most exercises, bodybuilders, and athletes who would like to up their energy but keep body fat down. A baked or steamed small to medium sweet potato can be a great post-workout snack.

2. Coconut Oil

This is a good fat full of "medium-chained" fats, which make it very easy to digest, as compared to other dietary fats. They are able to provide an easily accessible source of energy. Coconut oil is also a natural way to increase your metabolism, which gives your body the ability to burn more energy and boosts athletic performance. It also helps the function of the thyroid and gets rid of pancreatic stress, which will make you more active. You can easily add a couple of tablespoons into a smoothie.

3. Bananas

Bananas are a great source of potassium, which is an electrolyte that the body needs but loses when you are exercising. Appalachian State University did a study that found bananas were helpful in fueling cyclist during intense exercise. Bananas are also great at preventing muscle fatigue. Choosing a banana over an energy bar is much better options for some energy. They have a lot less sugar, and they have a lot more nutrients.

4. Rolled Oats

Oats are full of fiber, and they not only reduce your risk of developing heart disease, but they will also slow your glucose absorption, which will help to keep your energy up and your blood sugar levels steady. Oats also have a lot of B vitamins, which helps your body to change carbohydrates into usable energy.

5.   Walnuts

Since you won't be getting your Omega-3s from fish, walnuts should be your go-to. They are a great way to get those heart-healthy omega-3 fatty acids. Good fats are a very important part of your diet if you are serious about achieving optimal health and fitness. Healthy fats are able to help heal your body from bruises, sprains, and other tissue injuries, as well as aid in energy production. Unhealthy fats, on the other hand, can slow you down. Have a can of walnuts with your at all times just encase you start feeling sluggish, or, if you make your own trail mix, add in some walnuts.

6.   Lentils

Lentils are full of dietary fiber, containing eight grams in a half-cup serving. They are also great at keeping you feeling fuller for longer, and they will keep your energy levels up for your busy day.

7.   Coconut Water

If you are getting tired of drinking plain water, then you should try out some coconut water. There is only a mild coconut flavor, but it is full of important electrolytes. A lot of the sports drink on the market that have a lot of added sugars that play a part in diabetes and weight gain. Coconut water, on the other hand is a natural way to consume electrolytes with no additional sugars. You don't have to consume as much coconut water to get the beneficial minerals you need, so you won't end up feeling bloated or full like you would with other electrolyte drinks.

8.   Spinach

Spinach is full of folic acid and B vitamins, and both of these will provide you with lots of energy. Spinach can easily be added into different meals, from smoothies to scrambles and casseroles.

9.   Oranges

If you need a quick boost of energy, oranges should be your go-to food. It is full of natural sugars, and they will also give you three grams of fiber, which can help to sustain your energy levels. A single navel orange will help you to meet your daily requirement for vitamin C.

10.   Avocados

This delicious fruit is a great source of healthy fats that can activate your body. Your body can also utilize it for fuel to help you through your day or workout. It is also a great source of B6, folic acid, vitamin K, fiber, and vitamin C. Vitamin C is a great antioxidant that will help to support your adrenal glands, which you can end up overworking during stressful times. While B vitamins help with several functions within the body, they are often seen as the "stress and energy" vitamins. During a workout, your body becomes very stressed, so avocados work like a magic fruit.

11.   Olive Oil

Olive oil is praised all of the time for its health-promoting properties. It can help increase your healthy cholesterol levels, protect your blood vessels, and fight off free-radical damage. Most athletes who push themselves to the limit each and every day have to consume large amounts of calories to keep up with all of the energy they use, so try to add in a couple of tablespoons of EVOO to food that you have already cooked can help add some nutrient-dense calories and healthy fats.

12.   Matcha

This is a powdered form of green tea, but matcha tends to be better for you than regular green tea. It has five times the amount of l-theanine, which is an amino acid that promotes a focused and relaxed mental state. While matcha does have caffeine, like every other green tea, it contains enough l-theanine to get rid of the jitters that caffeine can cause for some people. That means you get high energy and intense focus without all of those ticks. Coffee does have some health benefits, but green tea also contains a lot of antioxidants that will help you to protect yourself from oxidative stress and fend off disease. Add a half of a teaspoon of matcha to six to eight ounces of hot water or steamed milk.

13. Acai Berries

This is a fruit that is native to South and Central America and is high in antioxidants, phytonutrients, minerals, and vitamins. These are things that can help you to fight off disease. Acai berries can help your body when you are exercising and provides you a natural source for sugar. It is a great choice over those sugar sports gels that don't contain important minerals and vitamins.

14. Kale

Everybody knows kale is a big player in the health food department. It is full of dietary fiber, manganese, calcium, vitamin C, and K, and it should be a staple in any bodybuilder's diet. It is considered a superfood and can increase yourathleticism due to its antioxidant levels. The antioxidants in kale can increase your blood oxygen, which will increase your physical stamina.

15. Raisins

This is an easily portable snack that can help to minimize inflammation and provide you with antioxidants. Look at raisins as a healthy carb option that will give you energy for those hard workouts. Add in some to your trail mix if you want.

16. Apricots

The last food on this list is apricots. There are some people who believe if they don't eat before a workout, they will end up burning more fat. While this may be true in some instances, it can also cause people to become dizzy, nausea, and lack important energy, which will hinder your ability to get the workout you want. Having a simple snack of an apricot before you workout can help give you the nutrients you need as well as an easily digested fuel to prevent all of those nasty side effects.

If you make sure you consume these energy-producing foods, along with others, you will never be lacking in energy or vitality. And, since you were a bodybuilder first, you should easily be able to slide into a plant-based diet that is full of these healthy energy-inducing foods without having to think about it.

Muscles And Proteins With Plant Based Diet

Protein Intake For Muscle Building

Understanding protein intake for muscle building on a plant-based diet

Healthy protein is not just crucial for a healthy and balanced diet plan and a smooth operating body; however, it is likewise a champ at developing and reinforcing muscular tissue mass.

While several individuals are mindful of animal-based resources of healthy protein, there are really a host of unbelievably varied, healthy and balanced, and effective all-natural plant-based resources. Plant-based proteins are not only merely as efficient as animal resources of healthy protein, they additionally provide the body with vitamins, minerals, and various other abundant nutrients (such as antioxidants, flavonoids, and polyphenols). Keeping that claimed, even if you recognize where you pick to gather your healthy protein, just how much suffices? Just how much is way too much? Is there an appropriate proportion to optimize your muscular tissue enhancing ventures?

The response is, of course, to all! To aid you in discovering your ideal protein-muscle proportion, continue reading and get all the information you need!

Why Is Protein Essential For Muscles

Healthy protein is one of the 3 macronutrients - materials that "give calories for power" - that are necessary for your body: carbs, fat, and healthy protein. When it comes to healthy protein, every gram provides up to 4 calories, and 15 percent of your weight is made of up of these grams of healthy protein.

What is healthy protein best at? It is best to create the structure of muscular tissue mass. Healthy proteins are real "structure blocks of muscular tissue mass," implying you cannot construct solid muscular tissues without sufficient resources of healthy and balanced protein.

Exactly How Does It Function?

It does not just fix, it additionally loads in the injury and making it "larger and more powerful," and as a result, developing even more muscular tissue mass. If your body does not have sufficient healthy protein to fix the splits, your body cannot construct more muscular tissue mass.

Learning More About Your Complete Proteins

While any plant-based food that is abundant in healthy protein benefits your muscle mass, there is a group described as "full healthy proteins" or "optimal healthy proteins" that are incredibly proficient at developing muscular tissue.

Hemp healthy protein - that "comes from the hemp plant, which does not have THC (the energetic component in cannabis)" - is vegan-friendly, easily offered at your neighborhood grocery store, and is packed complete of lean, healthy protein. One cup of raw soybeans contains an amount of 67 grams of healthy protein, while a cup of steamed soybeans provides 28 grams of healthy protein.

Best protein-rich plant-based foods for muscle strengthening

Per the USDA, it is essential to comply with 2 standards when picking healthy proteins for a well-balanced, healthy and well-adjusted, muscle mass structure diet plan: pick leaner and extra diverse, healthy proteins. The checklist of plant-based healthy protein choices is long, varied, and vivid.

Below are several of the leading protein-rich resources:

- Navy Beans (20 grams per cup).
- Chickpeas (7.25 grams per 1/2 cup).
- Lentils (13 grams per cup).
- Peanut Butter (8 grams per tbsp).
- Almonds (16.5 grams per 1/2 cup).
- Quinoa (8 grams per 1-cup offering).
- Edamame (8 grams per half-cup offering).
- Soba Noodles (12 grams per 3-ounce offering).

- Spirulina (8 grams per 2 tbsps).
- Chia Seeds (2 grams per tbsp).
- Hemp Seeds (5 grams per tbsp).
- Potatoes (8 grams per offering).
- Tofu (10 grams per 1/2 cup for company tofu).
- Tempeh (15 grams per 1/2 cup).
- Seitan (21 grams per 1/3 cup).

Keeping that stated, set your preferred vegetable with among the above protein-rich choices, and you are not just offering your body adequate healthy protein yet various other crucial nutrients and minerals.

Recognizing The Protein To Muscle Ratio

You'll listen to some clashing information when it comes to healthy protein intake versus muscular tissue conditioning or structure muscular tissue mass. This results from the truth that several aspects play into just how promptly or gradually each private body will certainly accumulate muscle mass. Age, sex, exercise levels, kind of exercise, selection of exercise, sources of healthy protein, the quantity of healthy protein, and when you are taking in healthy protein are just a few of these variables.

Without employing a costly individual fitness instructor or nutritional expert, how do you individuate the ideal equilibrium of healthy protein to the physical task to personal private variables?

Discovering Your Perfect Protein Ratio

Seeking advice from a specialist is a great idea. A few of us do not have the opportunity for numerous factors. All you require to recognize are a couple of straightforward standards that you can use to your circumstance, in brief, the healthy protein to bodyweight proportion!

Whether you are looking to gain muscular tissue mass, or merely straighten yourself, you will increase your healthy protein consumption, as it logically suggests much more muscle tissue.

This is not the case

Consuming over the advised quantity of healthy protein might be dangerous. For the ordinary adult, day-to-day healthy protein intake is around "0.37 grams per extra pound of body weight, and that amounts to about 56 grams of complete healthy protein for a 150-pound grownup."

When you have reached your objective using the 10 to 35 percent criteria, you can, after that, eat healthy protein in a modest and regular method utilizing the 0.37 grams per extra pound of bodyweight standard.

All Proteins In Plant Based Diet

Plant-Based Protein Filled Diet

There's a lengthy listing of veggies that contain sufficient quantities of healthy protein, though just a handful are "complete," suggesting that they include all the 9 of the essential amino acids discovered in healthy animal proteins. If you consume a healthy, vegetable-centric diet plan, you can definitively take pleasure in dishes that contain a high level of healthy protein.

The plant-based diet plan is very easy to follow as it is centered around foods originated from plant resources. Plant-based diet plans applaud on the consummation of fruits, veggies, whole grains, nuts, seeds, and vegetables, suggesting these foods should be the majority of what you consume. To provide you some pointers, our icy veggies are a basic yet tasty place to begin if you are aiming to gradually include even more plants into your lifestyle without making the complete transition in one go.

It is not just a plant-based diet regimen, it is a lot more adaptable and does not boycott milk, meat, fish and shellfish, and eggs completely. And what's even more, flexitarian diet plans advertise eating a vast selection of plant foods, so there are in a program to be adopted in many dietary plans as it gives many advantages.

As a country, we presently have a hard time staying up to date with this number of different diets, nonetheless, with a plant-based diet plan greatly relying upon vegetables and fruit, you are most likely to find it less complicated to eat the advised quantity of food and protein. As smoothies and beans are considerably energizing, you are expected to have a boosted consumption of fiber, vitamins, and minerals – this is very good as many of us are not eating enough fiber! To give you an idea of just how well veggies house a range of dietary advantages, peas offer healthy protein, fiber, folic acid, and vitamin C. It is all-natural to assume that a plant-based diet regimen can bring about an absence of healthy protein, yet this is far from the truth - plants give lots of healthy protein!

If you are attempting to move in the direction of an even more plant-based diet plan, I would suggest you try to get innovative and try out brand-new flavors and mixes that you have never attempted before!

These foods can aid you to satisfy your healthy protein requirements while supplying lots of taste, macronutrients, and various other nutrients required for a healthy and balanced diet regimen.

Plant-based consuming can imply a lot of changes in your life. Generally speaking, plant-based foods are those that focus on - you thought it - plants, and are reduced in animal-derived products such as meat, dairy products, fowl, fish, and eggs.

Deciding to alter your consuming practices is an individual choice, and one just you can make. Whether you are vegetarian, vegan, or a meat fan, upping your consumption of plant-based foods is a healthy and balanced option. Plant-based diet regimens are connected to a reduced threat of weight problems, cardiovascular disease, kind 2 diabetes mellitus, Alzheimer's, and some cancers cells.

Plant Based Supplements

Bodybuilding is extreme and drains the body faster than any other physical activity. A simple diet can provide much-needed energy and nutrients but it is not enough to maximize the muscle potential that is required for bodybuilding and athletics. Therefore, special supplements are needed to boost muscle growth. Since most of the protein supplements commonly available in the market are animal-sourced, they should be avoided. However, there are specific options for vegans:

1. Protein powder

Protein powder is extracted from plant-based sources and is an easier way to meet all protein needs as well as maintain net muscle protein balance. Protein powder can be mixed in smoothies, baked goods, and desserts. The commonly recommended plant-based protein powders include:

- Sunwarrior protein powder
- Vega protein powder
- Garden of Life
- PlantFusion

These supplements should be used with care, in an adequate amount.

2. BCAAs

Branch Chain Amino Acids, or BCAAs, are the types of amino acids that our body cannot produce on its own, so it needs to be consumed from external sources. Although BCAAs are also present in most of the plant-based proteins, it is always good to have some backup source for the hard training days. It can be consumed before or after the exercises and the workout sessions. They help in quick and improved recovery of the muscles after the exercise and help maintain the glycogen reserves. Buy yourself supplements which have a higher leucine to valine and isoleucine ratio (amino acids).

3. Creatine

Studies have shown that muscle strength and mass can be maximized by creatine. Creatine is largely found in animal-based sources. However, it is also producing by the human liver in some amount. Vegans have therefore comparatively lower levels of creatine in their blood. This level can be enhanced by supporting the liver function with a healthy diet and by taking supplements like Optimal Nutrition.

4.   NAC

NAC, or N-acetylcysteine, is a cysteine amino acid, and it is a comparatively stable form of protein that is easily absorbed in the body. NAC is discovered as that miraculous amino acid which can increase physical performance and reduces the oxidative stress of the cells. It is responsible for increasing levels of glutathione in the body.

5.   Ashwagandha

Indian ginseng, or ashwagandha, is full of healing benefits. Its tea is famous in traditional Indian cuisine due to the obvious advantages. This herb has also been used as medicine in most parts of the world. If you are looking for a natural supplement to boost your muscle recovery, then do add ashwagandha powder to your smoothies every now and then.

This herb has the ability to boost the production of testosterone in males by 15%, which helps to greatly increase in muscle strength and mass. It is both available in powder and pill forms.

This supplement can also reduce anxiety and stress due to the cortisol and c-reactive proteins. Superfoods Organic Ashwagandha root powder is recommended.

Cheat Days

It is important to give yourself a break from a diet in order to gain consistency. Most people give up on a diet because they become too hard on themselves. Cheat days are a way to keep yourself on track and curb your cravings. However, there are certain cheat day mistakes that cost too much for a bodybuilder who has worked hard to get his body in shape. Those common mistakes are:

1.   Frequent Cheating

2.   Excessive eating on the cheating days

3.   Too much dietary fat intake

4.   Drinking too much alcohol and sugary beverages

Even on your cheat days, keep your vegan lifestyle in mind and remind yourself of the caloric needs of the body. Cheating frequently and eating too much unhealthy food can get you off track, and can cause greater weight gain than usual. During your cheat days you can have things like:

1. Vegan ice creams
2. Protein bars
3. Cauliflower-crusted pizza
4. Vegan cookies

Management And Fitness Goals

Muscle growth and maintenance is all about management. Set your fitness goals and then follow the diet to meet those specific targets. Divide your goals into small achievable targets and then see the results. Here are some important points to keep in mind:

1. Self-discipline

It all starts with self-discipline; without you taming your mind, you cannot tame your body into a desired size and shape. The vegan bodybuilder must realize that this diet is as beneficial as any other animal-based diet. We just need to focus on the nutritional intake and must learn to maintain the proportion of the ingredients to meet the protein and caloric needs of the body.

2. Frequent and small meals

An effective strategy to keep the body fat free, maintain body weight, and increase muscle mass is to reduce the size of the meal and increase the frequency of daily meals. Each meal should carry more proteins than carbs and fats. It should also have a mix of all the essential micronutrients. With small and frequents meals, you constantly provide energy to the muscles to repair and rebuild while keeping the overall body weight maintained.

3. Grams per body weight

In the vegan bodybuilding diet, the important thing is to consider the proportion of nutrients in comparison to body weight. Perhaps, in this diet, there is no one-size-fits-all formula. Rather, every bodybuilder must consume proteins and other macronutrients as per the body's needs and weight. Consume proteins according to your body weight and size to maximize muscle growth.

4.   Calories

During strenuous exercises, our muscles burn a large number of calories to gain energy, which creates a constant demand for energy. Even when the muscles repair themselves, they need the energy to do so. Therefore, it is important to keep the caloric intake in check. Excessive calories are also not suitable for bodybuilders as it may lead to weight gain; the balance should be maintained.

5.   30% fat only

The total fat intake should only constitute 30% of the meal. This percentage is a standard limit for all. A higher fat intake would lead to the deposition of fats in the body and leads to obesity; 30% fat is enough to meet the basic fat needs of a body and prevents weight gain and other related problems.

6.   Consistent efforts

Just exercise and physical activities cannot guarantee good health and strong muscles—that has to be supported by a consistent effort and good diet. A person on a weight control diet has to be more cautious of his food preferences, portion size, and the bodily consumption of that food. Without consistency, all efforts are vain.

Breakfast Recipes

High-Protein Delicious Recipes For A Plant-Based Bodybuilding

This meal plan is a little higher in calories than our regular vegan athlete plan because it is designed to fuel your needs and muscle growth. Try our plant-based diet to build muscle like plants!

Mexican-Spiced Tofu Scramble

Preparation time: 13 m

Cooking time: 10 m

Ingredients:

1 tbsp. safflower oil

2 packages of extra-firm tofu, drained and pressed

3 scallions, chopped

2 cloves garlic, minced

1 red bell pepper, chopped

½ tsp. ground cumin

½ tsp. Mexican chile powder

½ tsp. ground coriander

½ tsp. paprika

½ tsp. garlic powder

½ tsp. dried oregano

1 tsp. black salt

2 tbsp. nutritional yeast (optional)

1/2 tsp. turmeric

2 tbsp. fresh cilantro, chopped

2 tbsp. ground flaxseed (optional)

1-4 oz. can green chiles

1 cup of water

1-15 oz. can black beans, drained and rinsed

Directions:

Heat a large frying pan over moderate heat. Add the oil and cook the chives, peppers, and garlic for about 3 minutes until tender. Break the tofu into large pieces and add them to the pan. Throw it away so that it is covered with aromatics and let it sit until it is golden before playing it. When browning after about 5 minutes, stir in the tofu to brown it on all sides.

While the tofu is browning, mix the spices in a small bowl or cup. Increase or reduce the amount depending on how you like spicy foods. Nutritional yeast and flax seeds are optional additions, but healthy if you have them. Add the spice blend to the pan and mix the tofu to evenly distribute the spices. Add 1 cup of water into the pan and stir. This helps the spices to distribute evenly and moistens the dispute. The water will cook.

Mix the green peppers and black beans in the tofu race. Cook for about 5 minutes until all the ingredients are hot. Mix the coriander. Serve hot.

Nutrition: Carbs: 91 g Calories: 1,113 Fat: 49 g Sodium: 670 mg Protein: 83 g Sugar: 9 g

Whole Grain Protein Bowl

Preparation time: 10 m

Cooking time: 0 m

Ingredients:

1 sliced banana

1/3 cup whole grains (like millet, couscous, quinoa, oat groats, etc.) cooked in 2/3 cup water

1 tablespoon nut butter

2 tablespoons dried goji berries

1 tablespoon raw sweetener (or throw in some dates or raisins)

3 tablespoons dried coconut chunks

1 tablespoon cacao nibs

Directions:

Throw it all together and eat!

Healthy Breakfast Bowl

Preparation time: 10 m

Cooking time: 10 m

Ingredients:

1 vegan yogurt

1/2 avocado (peeled and diced)

1 handful blueberries

1 tablespoon cacao nibs

1 handful of strawberries

1 tablespoon mulberries

1 tablespoon goji berries

1 tablespoon desiccated coconut

Directions:

Put the avocado in a nice bowl.

Top up with vegan yogurt.

Sprinkle the remaining ingredients and enjoy it.

Nutrition: carbohydrates: 55 g calories: 471 Fat: 25g sodium: 183 g protein: 11 g sugar: 32 g

Root Vegetable Hash With Avocado Crème

Preparation time: 25 m

Cooking time: 10 m

Ingredients:

1/2 c onion, diced

1 T vegan butter

2 cloves garlic, minced

1 c sweet potatoes, diced

1 c turnips, diced

1 c broccoli florets, diced

2 vegan sausages, diced

1 c collard greens, chopped

1/2 tsp sea salt

1 tsp cumin

1/2 tsp black pepper

1/4 – 1/2c vegetable stock

1/4 c fresh cilantro, chopped

1 medium avocado

1 T balsamic vinegar

1/4 c cashews

Directions:

Melt and hest the butter in a skillet. Add onion and garlic and sauté until they are translucent about 5 minutes.

Add sweet potatoes and turnips stir to match. Cook for 5-8 minutes.

Add the broccoli and vegetables. Continue cooking until it turns light green and start to soften for 5 to 8 minutes.

Add the roasted field, salt, pepper, cumin, coriander, and vinegar. Reduce the heat and get it cooked until the meat is hot and the flavors melt.

Mix the avocado, cashews, and vegetable broth in a blender until smooth.

Plate and serve with a spoonful of avocado cream on top. Garnish with more cilantro.

Nutrition: 19 g fat 30 g of carbohydrates 17 g protein 7 g sugar 691 mg sodium

Chocolate Strawberry Almond Protein Smoothie

Preparation time: 10 m

Cooking time: 10 m

Ingredients:

1 cup of organic strawberries

1 1/2 cup homemade almond milk

1 scoop chocolate protein powder

1 tablespoon organic coconut oil

1/4 cup organic raw almonds

1 tablespoon organic hemp seeds

1 tablespoon organic maca powder

For Garnish:

organic cacao nibs

organic hemp seeds

Directions:

Put all the ingredients inside a blender and beat until they are well combined.

Optional: Garnish with organic hemp seeds or organic cocoa beans.

Enjoy it!

Nutrition: carbohydrates: 39 g calories: 720 Fat: 45 g sodium: 732g protein: 44 g sugar: 12g

Banana Bread Breakfast Muffins

Preparation time: 40 m

Cooking time: 20 m

Ingredients:

1/2 cup plus 2 tbs of whole oats

1/2 cup oats (processed into flour)

1/2 teaspoon baking powder

2 tablespoon vegan chocolate chips

1/4 teaspoon cinnamon

1/2 cup of a mashed ripe banana (mash the banana and then measure it)

2 tablespoons pure maple syrup

1/2 teaspoon vanilla extract

Directions:

Preheat the cooker to 360 ° F and spray a muffin pan (3-4 holes) with a non-stick spray.

Add 1/2 cup oatmeal in a food processor and beat until it breaks and forms a thick consistency of flour.

In a large container, add all the dry ingredients except the chocolate chips and mix.

Crush and mash the uneven ripe banana, add the banana and the rest of the wet ingredients to the container with the dry ingredients and mix well.

Mix the chocolate chips. Put in 3-4 muffin holes and bake for 12 minutes.

Let cool 10 mins and serve immediately or store in an airtight container for 1-2 days.

Nutrition: Per serving: Carbohydrates: 59g Calories: 347 Fat: 6g Sodium: 2 mg Proteins: 15g Sugar: 1g

Stracciatella Muffins

Preparation time: 30 m

Cooking time: 15 m

Ingredients:

1 tablespoon vinegar

1 cup of soy milk

8 1/2-ounces flour

3/4-ounce grams brown sugar

3 1/2-ounces white sugar

2 packs of vanilla sugar

1/2 teaspoon salt

1 package baking soda

5-ounces vegan chocolate chip or finely grated chocolate (bittersweet)

2 tablespoons oil

Directions:

Preheat the oven to 355 ° F.

Mix the soy milk together with the vinegar and set aside.

In a large bowl, pour the flour, sugar, vanilla sugar, baking powder, and salt. Add the soybean oil and milk and mix until you get a smooth paste (with a spoon, not the blender).

Carefully fold the chocolate chips. Divide into 12 prepared muffin shapes and bake for 18 to 20 minutes until a toothpick comes out without sticky dough residue.

Nutrition: Per serving: Carbohydrates: 26 g Calories: 132 Fat: 7g Sodium: 17 mg Proteins: 2 g Sugar: 15 g

Cardamom Persimmon Scones With Maple-Persimmon Cream

Preparation time: 45 m

Cooking time: 30 m

Ingredients:

For the Dry Ingredients:

2 teaspoons baking powder

1 tablespoon coconut sugar

1 teaspoon cardamom

1/2 teaspoon salt

1/2 teaspoon cinnamon

3 tablespoons softened coconut oil

For the Wet Ingredients:

1/2 cup almond milk

1 teaspoon vanilla extract

1 cup plain vegan yogurt

1 teaspoon apple cider vinegar (if you use vegan yogurt)

1 cup ripe Fuyu persimmons chopped

For the Maple Cream:

2 tablespoons shredded coconut

1/2 cup chopped persimmons

3/4 cup non-dairy milk

1/4 teaspoon cinnamon

1 tablespoon maple syrup

1/4 teaspoon salt

Directions:

For Scones:

Preheat the cooker to 400 ° F. Line a baking sheet with parchment paper or leave it bare.

Combine flour, sugar, spices, baking soda, and salt in a large bowl.

Using a fork or pasta cutter, cut the coconut oil into the mixture.

Combine yogurt, almond milk, apple cider vinegar, and vanilla in a small bowl. Add the dey ingredients to the wet ingredients and stir with a wooden spoon until the mixture is well combined. Be careful not to mix too much.

Gently fold the chopped persimmons with the wooden spoon.

Flour on a flat surface like a board or a counter. Make the dough in a circle about 1.2 cm high. Cut into 8 slices and separate.

Carefully transfer the slices to the prepared baking sheet.

Bake at 400 ° F for 18 to 20 minutes. Let cool slightly before serving.

For the cream:

Combine all the constituents in a blender or food processor.

Serve with hot scones or refrigerate for up to 3 days.

Nutrition: Per serving: Carbohydrates: 45g Calories: 264 Fat: 7g Sodium: 46 mg Proteins: 6g Sugar: 15g

Activated Buckwheat & Coconut Porridge With Blueberry Sauce

Preparation time: 10 m

Cooking time: 5 m

Ingredients:

For the Porridge:

1/2 cup coconut milk

1 and 1/2 cups soaked and washed buckwheat

2 tablespoons rice malt syrup

1/2 teaspoon cinnamon

2 tablespoons coconut oil

1/2 teaspoon natural vanilla essence

For the Blueberry Sauce:

1 tablespoon rice malt syrup

1 cup blueberries (if you are using frozen, ensure they have defrosted)

3-4 tablespoons of water or coconut water

For the Toppings:

Banana

Roast coconut flakes

Directions:

Using a high-speed mixer or food processor, mix all the ingredients for the porridge and pour it into the bowl.

Clean and mix the blueberry sauce (if not mixed well, you may need to add more water, but you don't want it to drip)

Blueberry sauce in a buckwheat porridge, and with a spoon, you can make your whirlwind.

Add toppings and enjoy your healthy breakfast!

Nutrition: Per serving: Carbohydrates: 118g Calories: 738 Fat: 26g Sodium: 24 mg Proteins: 20g Sugar: 25g

Sweet Molasses Brown Bread

Preparation time: 1 hr 30 m

Cooking time: 30 m

Ingredients:

1/2 cup molasses

1 1/2 cups almond milk, warmed

4 tablespoons coconut oil or non-dairy butter, softened

1 2/3 cups white whole-wheat flour (or regular whole wheat flour)

3 cups unbleached of all-purpose flour, plus more for dusting

2 – 3 tablespoons unsweetened cocoa powder

1/2 teaspoon ground nutmeg

2 tablespoons dark brown sugar

1 1/4 teaspoons salt

Old-fashioned rolled oats for spray on top, optional

2 1/2 teaspoons instant yeast

Directions:

Combine dry ingredients, including yeast in a large bowl, make a hole in the mixture. Add the milk, molasses, and butter and mix with a wooden spoon until the dough is damp and unkempt, then knead by hand until the dough is thick.

Put the dough in a large bowl of oil (or leave it in a bread bucket); cover with a plastic wrap or cloth and let rise in a warm place until its size doubles, about 1 hour.

Turn the dough onto a surface that has been floured, divide it into 3 pieces, and mold it into bread.

Place the dough in a lightly greased baking sheet (or lined with parchment paper) or place it in greased forms and sprinkle with oatmeal.

Let the dough rise, protected in a warm place for 45 minutes to an hour until almost doubled in size.

Meanwhile, preheat the oven to 350 F. at the end of the rise time.

Bake for 25 to 30 mins until the color is darker , and a toothpick or tester inserted in the center comes out clean.

Remove the bread from the cooker and let cool in a rack.

Serve warm or at room temperature

Enjoy it!

Nutrition: carbohydrates: 584g calories: 3141 Fat: 63g sodium: 321 mg protein: 63g sugar: 171g

Lunch Recipes

Teriyaki Tofu Stir-Fry

Preparation time: 10 minutes

Cooking Time: 20 minutes

Serving: 4

Ingredients:

For the Tofu:

2 tablespoons chopped green onions

2 cups asparagus

14 ounces (397 grams) tofu, firm, pressed

2 teaspoons red chili sauce

1 tablespoon soy sauce

3 teaspoons olive oil

For the Sauce:

2 tablespoons minced garlic

1 ½ tablespoons rice vinegar

1/2 tablespoon grated ginger

2 teaspoons corn starch

1/4 cup (59 grams) coconut sugar

3 tablespoons soy sauce

1 tablespoon sesame oil

1/2 cup (118 ml) water

For Serving:

4 cups (946 grams) quinoa, cooked

Directions:

Prepare the tofu: pat dry tofu and cut into ½-inch cubes.

Take a medium skillet pan, place it over medium-high heat, add 1 teaspoon oil and when hot, add tofu cubes in a single layer, then cook for 3 to 4 minutes until golden brown.

Transfer tofu pieces to a large bowl, add 1 teaspoon oil in the pan and repeat with the remaining tofu cubes.

Meanwhile, prepare the sauce: take a small bowl, add all of the sauce ingredients in it and whisk until combined, then set aside until required.

When all the tofu gets cooked, drizzle them with sauces and toss until coated, set aside until required.

Wipe clean the skillet pan, return it over medium-high heat, add remaining oil and when hot, add asparagus and green onions, then cook for 3 minutes until tender-crisp.

Return tofu pieces into the pan, drizzle with prepared sauce, switch heat to medium level, toss until all the ingredients are mixed, and cook for 3 to 5 minutes until the sauce starts to thicken.

When done, taste to adjust the seasoning of the sauce and then remove the pan from heat.

Distribute cooked quinoa among plates, top with tofu and vegetables, and then serve.

Nutrition: 411 Cal; 11 g Fat; 1 g Saturated Fat; 58 g Carbs; 8 g Fiber; 19 g Protein; 12 g Sugar

Red Lentil And Quinoa Fritters

Preparation Time: 20 minutes

Cooking Time: 25 minutes

Serving: 10

Ingredients:

For the Fritters:

1/4 cup (59 grams) chickpea flour

1 ½ cups (354 grams) quinoa

1/4 cup (59 grams) cornmeal

1/2 cup (118 grams) red lentils

2 teaspoons ground turmeric

1/8 teaspoon black bell pepper

1/2 teaspoon salt

1/4 cup (59 grams) chopped parsley

1 teaspoon cumin

1/4 teaspoon ground cinnamon

1/2 of a lemon, juiced

1 tablespoon Dijon mustard

1/4 cup (59 grams) tahini

4 cups (946 ml) vegetable broth

For the Sauce:

1 teaspoon minced garlic

1/4 teaspoon salt

1 tablespoon chopped dill

3 tablespoons tahini

1 lemon, juiced

1 cup coconut yogurt, unsweetened

Directions:

Switch on the oven, set it to 400° F and let it preheat.

Take a medium pot, place it over medium-high heat, add lentils and quinoa, pour in vegetable broth, and bring it to a boil.

Switch heat to medium-low level and simmer the grains for 15 minutes until cooked, covering the pot.

When done, let grains cool for 10 minutes, fluff them with a fork and transfer into a large bowl.

Add remaining ingredients for the fritters in it and stir well until incorporated.

Shape the mixture into ten patties, arrange them on a baking sheet lined with aluminum foil and bake for 25 minutes until golden brown on both sides and thoroughly cooked, turning halfway.

Meanwhile, prepare the yogurt sauce: take a medium bowl, place all the ingredients for it inside and whisk until combined.

Serve fritters with yogurt sauce.

Nutrition: 173 Cal; 4 g Fat; 1 g Saturated Fat; 27 g Carbs; 2 g Fiber; 7 g Protein; 3 g Sugar;

Green Pea Fritters

Preparation Time: 10 minutes

Cooking Time: 25 minutes

Serving: 4

Ingredients:

For the Fritters:

1 ½ cups (140 grams) chickpea flour

2 cups (250 grams) frozen peas

1 large white onion, peeled, diced

1 tablespoon minced garlic

1/8 teaspoon salt

1 teaspoon baking soda

2 tablespoons mixed dried Italian herbs

1 tablespoon olive oil

Water as needed

For the Yoghurt Sauce:

1/2 teaspoon dried rosemary

1/2 teaspoon dried parsley

1/2 teaspoon dried mint

1 lemon, juiced

1 cup soy yogurt

Directions:

Switch on the oven, set it to 350° F and let it preheat.

Take a medium saucepan, place it over medium heat, add peas, cover them with water, bring it to a boil, cook for 2 to 3 minutes until tender, and when done, drain the peas and set aside until required.

Take a frying pan, place it over medium heat, add oil and when hot, add onion and garlic; cook for 5 minutes until softened.

Transfer onion-garlic mixture to a food processor, add peas and pulse for 1 minute until the thick paste comes together.

Tip the mixture in a bowl, add salt, baking soda, Italian herbs, and chickpea flour, stir until incorporated and shape the mixture into ten patties.

Brush the patties with oil, arrange them onto a baking sheet and bake for 15 to 18 minutes until golden brown and thoroughly cooked, turning halfway.

Meanwhile, prepare the yogurt sauce: take a medium bowl, add all the ingredients for it and whisk until combined.

Serve fritters with prepared yogurt sauce.

Nutrition: 94 Cal; 2 g Fat; 0 g Saturated Fat; 14 g Carbs; 3 g Fiber; 4 g Protein; 2 g Sugar

Breaded Tofu Steaks

Preparation Time: 10 minutes

Cooking Time: 12 minutes

Serving: 4

Ingredients:

3 cups (750 grams) tofu, extra-firm, pressed

4 tablespoons tomato paste

2 ½ tablespoons minced garlic

1 cup (236 grams) panko breadcrumbs and more as needed

½ teaspoon ground black pepper

2 tablespoon maple syrup

2 tablespoon Dijon mustard

2 tablespoon soy sauce

4 tablespoons olive oil

2 tablespoon water

BBQ sauce for serving

Directions:

Prepare the tofu steaks: pat dry tofu and then cut them into four slices.

Prepare the sauce: take a medium bowl, add garlic, black pepper, maple syrup, mustard, tomato paste, soy sauce, and water; stir until combined.

Take a shallow dish and place bread crumbs on it.

Working on one tofu steak at a time, first coat it with prepared sauce, then dredge it with bread crumbs until evenly coated and place it on a plate.

Repeat with the remaining tofu slices.

Take a frying pan, place it over medium heat, pour oil in it and when hot, place a tofu steak inside and cook for 4 to 6 minutes per side until golden brown and cooked.

Transfer tofu steak to a plate and repeat with the remaining tofu steaks.

Serve tofu steaks with the BBQ sauce.

Nutrition: 419.4 Cal; 23.9 g Fat; 3.9 g Saturated Fat; 33.3 g Carbs; 4.3 g Fiber; 22.8 g Protein; 3 g Sugar;

Chickpea And Edamame Salad

Preparation Time: 40 minutes

Cooking Time: 0 minutes

Serving: 4

Ingredients:

For the Salad:

3 tablespoons dried cranberries

1/4 cup (59 grams) diced carrots

3/4 cup (177 grams) edamame soybeans

1/3 cup (78 grams) chopped green pepper

30 ounces (850 grams) cooked chickpeas

1/3 cup (78 grams) chopped red pepper

1/2 teaspoon minced garlic

For the Dressing:

1/4 teaspoon dried oregano

1 teaspoon coconut sugar

1/4 teaspoon dried basil

1/3 teaspoon ground black pepper

1/3 teaspoon salt

1/4 teaspoon dried rosemary

1 teaspoon white vinegar

2 tablespoons grape seed oil

2 tablespoons olive oil

Directions:

Prepare the salad: take a large salad bowl, place all salad ingredients in it and then toss until properly mixed.

Prepare the dressing: take a small bowl, place all dressing ingredients in it and then whisk until combined.

Drizzle dressing over salad and toss until well mixed.

Place the salad bowl in the refrigerator for at least 30 minutes until chilled, then serve.

Nutrition: 119.6 Cal; 1.9 g Fat; 0.1 g Saturated Fat; 20.8 g Carbs; 4.8 g Fiber; 6 g Protein; 1.1 g Sugar;

Thai Tofu And Quinoa Bowls

Preparation Time: 15 minutes

Cooking Time: 20 minutes

Serving: 4

Ingredients:

3/4 cup (177 grams) quinoa, cooked

1 cup (236 grams) frozen edamame, thawed

12 ounces (175 grams) tofu, extra-firm, pressed

2 medium carrots, grated

1 green onion, sliced

1/2 teaspoon minced garlic

2 teaspoons grated ginger

1/2 cup chopped cilantro

1/2 teaspoon red chili flakes

1 tablespoon soy sauce

2 teaspoons agave syrup

2 tablespoons lime juice

2 tablespoons peanut butter

1 tablespoon water

4 teaspoons sesame seeds, toasted

Directions:

Switch on the oven, set it to 400° F and let it preheat.

Prepare the tofu: cut tofu into ¾-inch cubes.

Take a large baking sheet, line it with foil, spread tofu pieces on it, and bake for 20 minutes until golden brown, stirring halfway.

Prepare the drizzle: take a small bowl, place garlic, ginger, chili flakes, soy sauce, agave syrup, butter, lime, and water in it and then whisk until combined.

After tofu gets cooked, let it cool for 10 minutes and transfer into a large bowl.

Add carrot, green onions, cilantro, cabbage, and edamame, drizzle with the prepared dressing and sprinkle with sesame seeds.

Mix quinoa with salad and serve.

Nutrition: 330 Cal; 13 g Fat; 3 g Saturated Fat; 36 g Carbs; 7 g Fiber; 19 g Protein; 10 g Sugar;

Black Bean And Bulgur Chili

Preparation Time: 10 minutes

Cooking Time: 20 minutes

Serving: 4

Ingredients:

3/4 cup (177 grams) bulgur wheat, ground

30 ounces (850 grams) cooked black beans

1 medium red bell pepper, cored, diced

1 red onion, peeled, chopped

1 medium green bell pepper, cored, diced

1 chipotle pepper in adobo sauce, deseeded, diced

1 teaspoon minced garlic

1 teaspoon smoked paprika

1/8 teaspoon sea salt

1 teaspoon dried oregano

1 teaspoon ground cumin

3 cups (710 ml) vegetable broth

1 tablespoon olive oil

1 lime, juiced

1 ¼ cups (295 grams) enchilada sauce

For Topping:

1/2 cup (118 grams) chopped cilantro

Directions:

Take a large pot, place it over medium-low heat, add oil and when hot, add onion and garlic, season with salt, and cook for 3 minutes until softened.

Add bell peppers, continue cooking for 5 minutes until tender, add remaining ingredients and stir until mixed.

Bring the mixture to a boil, switch heat to a low level and simmer for 10 minutes.

Taste to adjust seasoning, then remove the pot from heat, cover it with lid and let it stand for 10 minutes.

Distribute chili among bowls, top with cilantro and serve.

Nutrition: 387 Cal; 6.5 g Fat; 1.2 g Saturated Fat; 67.5 g Carbs; 18.6 g Fiber; 19.8 g Protein; 6 g Sugar;

Cauliflower Steaks

Preparation Time: 10 minutes

Cooking Time: 30 minutes

Serving: 3

Ingredients:

2 medium heads of cauliflower

1 teaspoon garlic powder

1/2 teaspoon ground black pepper

1 teaspoon salt

1 teaspoon coriander

1 teaspoon paprika

2 tablespoons olive oil

For Serving:

1 cup (236 grams) hummus

Directions:

Switch on the oven, set it to 425° F and let it preheat.

Cut each cauliflower head into three slices, brush them with oil on both sides and sprinkle with garlic powder, black pepper, salt, coriander, and paprika.

Take a large baking sheet, line it with aluminum foil, arrange cauliflower steaks on it and then bake for 30 minutes until tender and golden brown on both sides.

Serve straight away.

Nutrition: 149 Cal; 9 g Fat; 1 g Saturated Fat; 14 g Carbs; 7 g Fiber; 5 g Protein; 3 g Sugar;

Avocado And Hummus Sandwich

Preparation Time: 5 minutes

Cooking Time: 0 minutes

Serving: 1

Ingredients:

2 slices of whole-wheat bread sliced

4 slices of tomato

1 lettuce leaf

1/2 avocado, sliced

2 tablespoons cilantro leaves

2 teaspoons hot sauce

3 tablespoon hummus

Directions:

Take a slice of bread, spread hummus on its one side, then top with avocado slices and drizzle with hot sauce.

Scatter tomato slice on top of avocado slices, then top with lettuce and cilantro and cover with the other slice of bread.

Serve straight away.

Nutrition: 302 Cal; 5.7 g Fat; 1.1 g Saturated Fat; 49.8 g Carbs; 12 g Fiber; 12.8 g Protein; 7.8 g Sugar;

Chickpea Spinach Salad

Preparation Time: 10 minutes

Cooking Time: 0 minutes

Serving: 2

Ingredients:

12 ounces (340 grams) cooked chickpeas

1/4 cup (59 grams) raisins

1 cup (236 grams) spinach

1/2 teaspoon red chili flakes

1/8 teaspoon salt

1 teaspoon cumin

3 teaspoons agave syrup

1/2 tablespoon lemon juice

4 tablespoons olive oil

3 ½ ounces (99 grams) vegan parmesan cheese

Directions:

Take a large salad bowl, add chickpeas and spinach in it, then add cheese and toss until mixed.

Prepare the dressing: take a small bowl, add raisins in it along with salt, pepper, cumin, lemon juice, agave syrup and oil and whisk until combined.

Drizzle the dressing over salad, toss until well coated, and serve.

Nutrition: 658 Cal; 40 g Fat; 11 g Saturated Fat; 52 g Carbs; 9.7 g Fiber; 23 g Protein; 15.2 g Sugar;

Dinner Recipes

Mushroom Steak

Preparation Time: 30 min.

Cooking Time: 1 hr.

Servings: 8

Ingredients:

1 tbsp. of the following:

fresh lemon juice

olive oil, extra virgin

2 tbsp. coconut oil

3 thyme sprigs

8 medium Portobello mushrooms

For Sauce:

1 ½ t. of the following:

minced garlic

minced peeled fresh ginger

2 tbsp. of the following:

light brown sugar

mirin

½ c. low-sodium soy sauce

Directions:

For the sauce, combine all the sauce ingredients, along with ¼ cup water into a little pan and simmer to cook. Cook using a medium heat until it reduces to a glaze, approximately 15 to 20 minutes, then remove from the heat.

For the mushrooms, bring the oven to 350 heat setting.

Using a skillet, melt coconut oil and olive oil, cooking the mushrooms on each side for about 3 minutes.

Next, arrange the mushrooms in a single layer on a sheet for baking and season with lemon juice, salt, and pepper.

Carefully slide into the oven and roast for 5 minutes. Let it rest for 2 minutes.

Plate and drizzle the sauce over the mushrooms.

Enjoy.

Nutrition: Calories: 87 | Carbohydrates: 6.2 g | Proteins: 3 g | Fats: 6.2 g

Spicy Grilled Tofu Steak

Preparation Time: 30 min.

Cooking Time: 20 min.

Servings: 4

Ingredients:

1 tbsp. of the following:

chopped scallion

chopped cilantro

soy sauce

hoisin sauce

2 tbsp. oil

¼ t. of the following:

salt

garlic powder

red chili pepper powder

ground Sichuan peppercorn powder

½ t. cumin

1 pound firm tofu

Directions:

Place the tofu on a plate and drain the excess liquid for about 10 minutes.

Slice drained tofu into ¾ thick stakes.

Stir the cumin, Sichuan peppercorn, chili powder, garlic powder, and salt in a mixing bowl until well-incorporated.

In another little bowl, combine soy sauce, hoisin, and 1 teaspoon of oil.

Heat a skillet to medium temperature with oil, then carefully place the tofu in the skillet.

Sprinkle the spices over the tofu, distributing equally across all steaks. Cook for 3-5 minutes, flip, and put spice on the other side. Cook for an additional 3 minutes.

Brush with sauce and plate.

Sprinkle some scallion and cilantro and enjoy.

Nutrition: Calories: 155 | Carbohydrates: 7.6 g | Proteins: 9.9 g | Fats: 11.8g

Piquillo Salsa Verde Steak

Preparation Time: 30 min.

Cooking Time: 25 min.

Yields: 8 Servings

Ingredients:

4 – ½ inch thick slices of ciabatta

18 oz. firm tofu, drained

5 tbsp. olive oil, extra virgin

Pinch of cayenne

½ t. cumin, ground

1 ½ tbsp. sherry vinegar

1 shallot, diced

8 piquillo peppers (can be from a jar) – drained and cut to ½ inch strips

3 tbsp. of the following:

parsley, finely chopped

capers, drained and chopped

Directions:

Place the tofu on a plate to drain the excess liquid, and then slice into 8 rectangle pieces.

You can either prepare your grill or use a grill pan. If using a grill pan, preheat the grill pan.

Mix 3 tablespoons of olive oil, cayenne, cumin, vinegar, shallot, parsley, capers, and piquillo peppers in a medium bowl to make our salsa verde. Season to preference with salt and pepper.

Using a paper towel, dry the tofu slices.

Brush olive oil on each side, seasoning with salt and pepper lightly.

Place the bread on the grill and toast for about 2 minutes using medium-high heat.

Next, grill the tofu, cooking each side for about 3 minutes or until the tofu is heated through.

Place the toasted bread on the plate then the tofu on top of the bread.

Gently spoon out the salsa verde over the tofu and serve.

Nutrition: Calories: 427 | Carbohydrates: 67.5 g | Proteins: 14.2 g | Fats: 14.6 g

Butternut Squash Steak

Preparation Time: 30 min.

Cooking Time: 50 min.

Servings: 4

Ingredients:

2 tbsp. coconut yogurt

½ t. sweet paprika

1 ¼ c. low-sodium vegetable broth

1 sprig thyme

1 finely chopped garlic clove

1 big thinly sliced shallot

1 tbsp. margarine

2 tbsp. olive oil, extra virgin

Salt and pepper to liking

Directions:

Bring the oven to 375 heat setting.

Cut the squash, lengthwise, into 4 steaks.

Carefully core one side of each squash with a paring knife in a crosshatch pattern.

Using a brush, coat with olive oil each side of the steak then season generously with salt and pepper.

In an oven-safe, non-stick skillet, bring 2 tablespoons of olive oil to a warm temperature.

Place the steaks on the skillet with the cored side down and cook at medium temperature until browned, approximately 5 minutes.

Flip and repeat on the other side for about 3 minutes.

Place the skillet into the oven to roast the squash for 7 minutes.

Take out from the oven, placing on a plate and covering with aluminum foil to keep warm.

Using the previously used skillet, add thyme, garlic, and shallot, cooking at medium heat.

Stir frequently for about 2 minutes.

Add brandy and cook for an additional minute.

Next, add paprika and whisk the mixture together for 3 minutes.

Add in the yogurt seasoning with salt and pepper.

Plate the steaks and spoon the sauce over the top.

Garnish with parsley and enjoy!

Nutrition: Calories: 300 | Carbohydrates: 46 g | Proteins: 5.3 g | Fats: 10.6g

Cauliflower Steak Kicking Corn

Preparation Time: 30 min.

Cooking Time: 60 min.

Servings: 6

Ingredients:

2 t. capers, drained

4 scallions, chopped

1 red chili, minced

¼ c. vegetable oil

2 ears of corn, shucked

2 big cauliflower heads

Salt and pepper to taste

Directions:

Heat the oven to 375 degrees.

Boil a pot of water, about 4 cups, using the maximum heat setting available.

Add corn in the saucepan, cooking approximately 3 minutes or until tender.

Drain and allow the corn to cool, then slice the kernels away from the cob.

Warm 2 tablespoons of vegetable oil in a skillet.

Combine the chili pepper with the oil, cooking for approximately 30 seconds.

Next, combine the scallions, sautéing with the chili pepper until soft.

Mix in the corn and capers in the skillet and cook for approximately 1 minute to blend the flavors. Then remove from heat.

Warm 1 tablespoon of vegetable oil in a skillet. Once warm, begin to place cauliflower steaks to the pan, 2 to 3 at a time. Season to your liking with salt and cook over medium heat for 3 minutes or until lightly browned.

Once cooked, slide onto the cookie sheet and repeat step 5 with the remaining cauliflower.

Take the corn mixture and press into the spaces between the florets of the cauliflower.

Bake for 25 minutes.

Serve warm and enjoy!

Nutrition: Calories: 153 | Carbohydrates: 15 g | Proteins: 4 g | Fats: 10 g

Pistachio Watermelon Steak

Preparation Time: 5 min.

Cooking Time: 10 min.

Servings: 4

Ingredients:

Microgreens

Pistachios chopped

Malden sea salt

1 tbsp. olive oil, extra virgin

1 watermelon

Salt to taste

Directions:

Begin by cutting the ends of the watermelon.

Carefully peel the skin from the watermelon along the white outer edge.

Slice the watermelon into 4 slices, approximately 2 inches thick.

Trim the slices, so they are rectangular in shape approximately 2 x4 inches.

Heat a skillet to medium heat add 1 tablespoon of olive oil.

Add watermelon steaks and cook until the edges begin to caramelize.

Plate and top with pistachios and microgreens.

Sprinkle with Malden salt.

Serve warm and enjoy!

Nutrition: Calories: 67 | Carbohydrates: 3.8 g | Proteins: 1.6 g Fats: 5.9 g

Bbq Ribs

Preparation Time: 30 min.

Cooking Time: 45 min.

Servings: 2

Ingredients:

2 drops liquid smoke

2 tbsp. of the following:

soy sauce

tahini

1 c. of the following:

water

wheat gluten

1 tbsp. of the following:

garlic powder

onion powder

lemon pepper

2 t. chipotle powder

For the Sauce:

2 chipotle peppers in adobo, minced

1 tbsp. of the following:

vegan Worcestershire sauce

lemon juice

horseradish

onion powder

garlic powder

ground pepper

1 t. dry mustard

2 tbsp. sweetener of your choice

5 tbsp. brown sugar

½ c. apple cider vinegar

2 c. ketchup

1 c. water

1 freshly squeezed orange juice

Directions:

Set the oven to 350 heat setting, and prepare the grill charcoal as recommended for this, but gas will work as well.

Combine soy sauce, tahini, water, and liquid smoke in a bowl. Then set this mixture to the side in a mixing bowl.

Next, use a big glass bowl to mix chipotle powder, onion powder, lemon pepper, garlic powder; combine well then whisk in the ingredients from the little bowl.

Add the wheat gluten and mix until it comes to a gooey consistency.

Grease a standard-size loaf pan and transfer the mixture to the loaf pan. Smooth it out so that the rib mixture fits flat in the pan.

Bake for 30 minutes.

While the mixture is baking, make the BBQ sauce. To make the sauce, combine all the sauce ingredients in a pot. Allow the mixture to simmer its way to the boiling point to combine the flavors, and as soon as it boils, decrease the heat to the minimum setting. Let it be for 10 more minutes.

Cautiously take the rib out of the oven and slide onto a plate.

Coat the top rib mixture with the BBQ Sauce and place on the grill.

Coat the other side of the rib mixture with BBQ Sauce and grill for 6 minutes

Flip and grill the other side for an additional 6 minutes.

Serve warm and enjoy!

Nutrition: Calories: 649 | Carbohydrates: 114 g | Proteins: 34.8 g | Fats: 11.1g

Spicy Veggie Steaks With Veggies

Preparation Time: 30 min.

Cooking Time: 45 mins.

Servings: 4

Ingredients:

1 ¾ c. vital wheat gluten

½ c. vegetable stock

¼ t. liquid smoke

1 tbsp. Dijon mustard

1 t. paprika

½ c. tomato paste

2 tbsp. soy sauce

½ t. oregano

¼ t. of the following:

coriander powder

cumin

1 t. of the following:

onion powder

garlic powder

¼ c. nutritional yeast

¾ c. canned chickpeas

Marinade:

½ t. red pepper flakes

2 cloves garlic, minced

2 tbsp. soy sauce

1 tbsp. lemon juice, freshly squeezed

¼ c. maple syrup

For skewers:

15 skewers, soaked in water for 30 minutes if wooden

¾ t. salt

8 oz. zucchini or yellow summer squash

¼ t. ground black pepper

1 tbsp. olive oil

1 red onion, medium

Directions:

In a food processor, add chickpeas, vegetable stock, liquid smoke, Dijon mustard, pepper, paprika, tomato paste, soy sauce, oregano, coriander, cumin, onion powder, garlic, and natural yeast. Process until the ingredients are well-mixed.

Add the vital wheat gluten to a big mixing bowl, and pour the contents from the food processor into the center. Mix with a spoon until a soft dough is formed.

Knead the dough for approximately 2 minutes; do not over knead.

Once the dough is firm and stretchy, flatten it to create 4 equal-sized steaks.

Individually wrap the steaks in tin foil; be sure not to wrap the steaks too tightly, as they will expand when steaming.

Steam for 20 minutes. To steam, you can use any steamer you like or a basket over boiling water.

While steaming, prepare the marinade. In a bowl, whisk the red pepper, garlic, soy sauce, lemon juice, and syrup. Reserve half of the sauce for brushing during grilling.

Prepare the skewers. Cut the onion and zucchini or yellow squash into 1/2-inch chunks.

In a glass bowl, add the red onion, zucchini, and yellow squash then coat with olive oil, pepper, and salt to taste. Place the vegetables on the skewers.

After the steaks have steamed for 20 minutes, unwrap and place on a cookie sheet. Pour the marinade over the steaks, fully covering them.

Bring your skewers, steaks, and glaze to the grill. Place the skewers on the grill over direct heat. Brush skewers with glaze. Grill for approximately 3 minutes then flip.

Place the steaks directly on the grill, glaze side down, and brush the top with additional glaze. Cook to your desired doneness.

Serve warm and enjoy!

Nutrition: Calories: 458 | Carbohydrates: 65.5 g | Proteins: 39.1 g | Fats: 7.6 g

Smoothies And Shakes and Desserts

Chocolate Smoothie

Preparation Time: 5 min.

Cooking Time: 5 min.

Servings: 2

Ingredients:

¼ c. almond butter

¼ c. cocoa powder, unsweetened

½ c. coconut milk, canned

1 c. almond milk, unsweetened

Directions:

Before making the smoothie, freeze the almond milk into cubes using an ice cube tray. This would take a few hours, so prepare it ahead.

Blend everything using your preferred machine until it reaches your desired thickness.

Serve immediately and enjoy!

Nutrition: Calories: 147 | Carbohydrates: 8.2 g | Proteins: 4 g | Fats: 13.4 g

Chocolate Mint Smoothie

Preparation Time: 5 min.

Cooking Time: 5 min.

Serving: 1

Ingredients:

2 tbsp. sweetener of your choice

2 drops mint extract

1 tbsp. cocoa powder

½ avocado, medium

¼ c. coconut milk

1 c. almond milk, unsweetened

Directions:

In a high-speed blender, add all the ingredients and blend until smooth.

Add two to four ice cubes and blend.

Serve immediately and enjoy!

Nutrition: Calories: 401 | Carbohydrates: 6.3 g | Proteins: 5 g | Fats: 40.3 g

Cinnamon Roll Smoothie

Preparation Time: 2 min.

Cooking Time: 2 min.

Serving: 1

Ingredients:

1 t. cinnamon

1 scoop vanilla protein powder

½ c. of the following:

• 	almond milk, unsweetened

• 	coconut milk

Sweetener of your choice

Directions:

In a high-speed blender, add all the ingredients and blend.

Add two to four ice cubes and blend until smooth.

Serve immediately and enjoy!

Nutrition: Calories: 507 | Carbohydrates: 17 g | Proteins: 33.3 g | Fats: 34.9 g

Coconut Smoothie

Preparation Time: 2 min.

Cooking Time: 2 min.

Servings: 2

Ingredients:

1 t. chia seeds

1/8 c. almonds, soaked

1 c. coconut milk

1 avocado

Directions:

In a high-speed blender, add all the ingredients and blend until smooth.

Add your desired number of ice cubes, depending on your favored consistency, of course, and blend again.

Serve immediately and enjoy!

Nutrition: Calories: 584 | Carbohydrates: 22.5 g | Proteins: 8.3 g | Fats: 55.5g

Maca Almond Smoothie

Preparation Time: 5 min.

Cooking Time: 5 min.

Servings: 2

Ingredients:

½ t. vanilla extract

1 scoop maca powder

1 tbsp. almond butter

1 c. almond milk, unsweetened

2 avocados

Directions:

In a high-speed blender, add all the ingredients and blend until smooth.

Serve immediately and enjoy!

Nutrition: Calories: 758 | Carbohydrates: 28.6 g | Proteins: 9.3 g | Fats: 72.3 g

Blueberry Smoothie

Preparation Time: 5 min.

Cooking Time: 5 min.

Serving: 1

Ingredients:

¼ c. pumpkin seeds shelled unsalted

3 c. blueberries, frozen

2 avocados, peeled and halved

1 c. almond milk

Directions:

In a high-speed blender, add all the ingredients and blend until smooth.

Add two to four ice cubes and blend until smooth.

Serve immediately and enjoy!

Nutrition: Calories: 401 | Carbohydrates: 6.3 g | Proteins: 5 g | Fats: 40.3 g

Nutty Protein Shake

Preparation Time: 5 min.

Cooking Time: 5 min.

Serving: 1

Ingredients:

¼ avocado

2 tbsp. powdered peanut butter

1 tbsp. of the following:

- Cocoa powder
- Peanut butter

1 scoop protein powder

½ c. almond milk

Directions:

In a high-speed blender, add all the ingredients and blend until smooth.

Add two to four ice cubes and blend again.

Serve immediately and enjoy!

Nutrition: Calories: 694 | Carbohydrates: 30.8 g | Proteins: 40.8 g | Fats: 52 g

Cinnamon Pear Smoothie

Preparation Time: 2 min.

Cooking Time: 2 min.

Serving: 1

Ingredients:

1 t. cinnamon

1 scoop vanilla protein powder

½ c. of the following:

Almond milk, unsweetened

Coconut Milk

2 pears, cores removed

Sweetener of your choice

Directions:

In a high-speed blender, add all the ingredients and blend.

Add two or more ice cubes and blend again.

Serve immediately and enjoy!

Nutrition: Calories: 653 | Carbohydrates: 75.2 g | Proteins: 28.4 g | Fats: 32.2 g

Vanilla Milkshake

Preparation Time: 5 min.

Cooking Time: 5 min.

Servings: 4

Ingredients:

2 c. ice cubes

2 t. vanilla extract

6 tbsp. powdered erythritol

1 c. cream of dairy-free

½ c. coconut milk

Directions:

In a high-speed blender, add all the ingredients and blend.

Add ice cubes and blend until smooth.

Serve immediately and enjoy!

Nutrition: Calories: 125 | Carbohydrates: 6.8 g | Proteins: 1.2 g | Fats: 11.5 g

Raspberry Protein Shake

Preparation Time: 5 min.

Cooking Time: 5 min.

Serving: 1

Ingredients:

¼ avocado

1 c. raspberries, frozen

1 scoop protein powder

½ c. almond milk

Ice cubes

Directions:

In a high-speed blender add all the ingredients and blend until lumps of fruit disappear.

Add two to four ice cubes and blend to your desired consistency.

Serve immediately and enjoy!

Nutrition: Calories: 756 | Carbohydrates: 80.1 g | Proteins: 27.6 g | Fats: 40.7 g

Raspberry Almond Smoothie

Preparation Time: 5 min.

Cooking Time: 5 min.

Serving: 1

Ingredients:

10 Almonds, finely chopped

3 tbsp. almond butter

1 c. almond milk

1 c. Raspberries, frozen

Directions:

In a high-speed blender, add all the ingredients and blend until smooth.

Serve immediately and enjoy!

Nutrition: Calories: 449 | Carbohydrates: 26 g | Proteins: 14 g | Fats: 35 g

Apple Raspberry Cobbler

Preparation Time: 50 minutes

Servings: 4

A safer type of fruit cobbler where a cut in sugar enhances the fruit.

Ingredients

3 apples, peeled, cored, and chopped

2 tbsp pure date sugar

1 cup fresh raspberries

2 tbsp unsalted plant butter

½ cup whole-wheat flour

1 cup toasted rolled oats

2 tbsp pure date sugar

1 tsp cinnamon powder

Directions

Preheat the oven to 350 F and grease a baking dish with some plant butter.

Add the apples, date sugar, and 3 tbsp of water to a medium pot. Cook over low heat until the date sugar melts and then, mix in the raspberries. Cook until the fruits soften, 10 minutes.

Pour and spread the fruit mixture into the baking dish and set aside.

In a blender, add the plant butter, flour, oats, date sugar, and cinnamon powder. Pulse a few times until crumbly.

Spoon and spread the mixture on the fruit mix until evenly layered.

Bake in the oven for 25 to 30 minutes or until golden brown on top.

Remove the dessert, allow cooling for 2 minutes, and serve.

Nutritional info per serving

Calories 539 | Fats 12g| Carbs 105.7g | Protein 8.2g

White Chocolate Pudding

Preparation Time: 4 hours 20 minutes

Servings: 4

Ingredients

3 tbsp flax seed + 9 tbsp water

3 tbsp cornstarch

¼ tbsp salt

1 cup cashew cream

2 ½ cups almond milk

½ pure date sugar

1 tbsp vanilla caviar

6 oz unsweetened white chocolate chips

Whipped coconut cream for topping

Sliced bananas and raspberries for topping

Directions

In a small bowl, mix the flax seed powder with water and allow thickening for 5 minutes to make the flax egg.

In a large bowl, whisk the cornstarch and salt, and then slowly mix in the in the cashew cream until smooth. Whisk in the flax egg until well combined.

Pour the almond milk into a pot and whisk in the date sugar. Cook over medium heat while frequently stirring until the sugar dissolves. Reduce the heat to low and simmer until steamy and bubbly around the edges.

Pour half of the almond milk mixture into the flax egg mix, whisk well and pour this mixture into the remaining milk content in the pot. Whisk continuously until well combined.

Bring the new mixture to a boil over medium heat while still frequently stirring and scraping all the corners of the pot, 2 minutes.

Turn the heat off, stir in the vanilla caviar, then the white chocolate chips until melted. Spoon the mixture into a bowl, allow cooling for 2 minutes, cover with plastic wraps making sure to press the plastic onto the surface of the pudding, and refrigerate for 4 hours.

Remove the pudding from the fridge, take off the plastic wrap and whip for about a minute.

Spoon the dessert into serving cups, swirl some coconut whipping cream on top, and top with the bananas and raspberries. Enjoy immediately.

Nutritional info per serving

Calories 654 | Fats 47.9g| Carbs 52.1g | Protein 7.3g

Ambrosia Salad With Pecans

Preparation Time: 15 minutes + 1 hour chilling

Servings: 4

These are the ingredients that inflict anguish if skipped at the celebration plate.

Ingredients

1 cup pure coconut cream

½ tsp vanilla extract

2 medium bananas, peeled and cut into chunks

1 ½ cups unsweetened coconut flakes

4 tbsp toasted pecans, chopped

1 cup pineapple tidbits, drained

1 (11 oz) can mandarin oranges, drained

¾ cup maraschino cherries, stems removed

Directions

In medium bowl, mix the coconut cream and vanilla extract until well combined.

In a larger bowl, combine the bananas, coconut flakes, pecans, pineapple, oranges, and cherries until evenly distributed.

Pour on the coconut cream mixture and fold well into the salad.

Chill in the refrigerator for 1 hour and serve afterwards.

Nutritional info per serving

Calories 648 | Fats 36g| Carbs 85.7g | Protein 6.6g

Peanut Butter Blossom Biscuits

Preparation Time: 15 minutes + 1 hour chilling

Servings: 4

Ingredients

1 tbsp flax seed powder + 3 tbsp water

1 cup pure date sugar + more for dusting

½ cup creamy peanut butter

1 tsp vanilla extract

1 ¾ cup whole-wheat flour

1 tsp baking soda

¼ tsp salt

¼ cup unsweetened chocolate chips

Directions

In a small bowl, mix the flax seed powder with water and allow thickening for 5 minutes to make the flax egg.

In a medium bowl using an electric mixer, whisk the date sugar, plant butter, and peanut butter until light and fluffy.

Mix in the flax egg and vanilla until well combined. Add the flour, baking soda, salt, and whisk well again.

Fold in the chocolate chips, cover the bowl with a plastic wrap, and refrigerate for 1 hour. After, preheat the oven to 375 F and line a baking sheet with parchment paper.

Use a cookie sheet to scoop mounds of the batter onto the sheet with 1-inch intervals. Bake in the oven for 9 to 10 minutes or until golden brown and slightly cracked on top.

Remove the cookies from the oven, cool for 3 minutes, roll in some date sugar, and serve.

Nutritional info per serving

Calories 839 | Fats 52.5g| Carbs 77.9g | Protein 21.1g

Chocolate & Almond Butter Barks

Preparation Time: 35 minutes

Servings: 4

Chewy fluffy almonds is equal to delicious almond bark, handmade dairy-free chocolate bars!

Ingredients

1/3 cup coconut oil, melted

¼ cup almond butter, melted

2 tbsp unsweetened coconut flakes.

1 tsp pure maple syrup

A pinch ground rock salt

¼ cup unsweetened cocoa nibs

Directions

Line a baking tray with baking paper and set aside.

In a medium bowl, mix the coconut oil, almond butter, coconut flakes, maple syrup, and then fold in the rock salt and cocoa nibs.

Pour and spread the mixture on the baking sheet, chill in the refrigerator for 20 minutes or until firm.

Remove the dessert, break into shards and enjoy immediately.

Preserve extras in the refrigerator.

Nutritional info per serving

Calories 279 | Fats 28.1g| Carbs 8.6g | Protein 4.4g

Mini Berry Tarts

Preparation Time: 35 minutes + 1 hour chilling

Servings: 4

Tickle-sized berries-filled with surprises, oh so delicious! Also so delicious that you can't stop having them.

Ingredients

For the piecrust:

4 tbsp flax seed powder + 12 tbsp water

1/3 cup whole-wheat flour + more for dusting

½ tsp salt

¼ cup plant butter, cold and crumbled

3 tbsp pure malt syrup

1 ½ tsp vanilla extract

For the filling:

6 oz cashew cream

6 tbsp pure date sugar

¾ tsp vanilla extract

1 cup mixed frozen berries

Directions

Preheat the oven to 350 F and grease a mini pie pans with cooking spray.

In a medium bowl, mix the flax seed powder with water and allow soaking for 5 minutes.

In a large bowl, combine the flour and salt. Add the butter and using an electric hand mixer, whisk until crumbly. Pour in the flax egg, malt syrup, vanilla, and mix until smooth dough forms.

Flatten the dough on a flat surface, cover with plastic wrap, and refrigerate for 1 hour.

After, lightly dust a working surface with some flour, remove the dough onto the surface, and using a rolling pin, flatten the dough into a 1-inch diameter circle,

Use a large cookie cutter, cut out rounds of the dough and fit into the pie pans. Use a knife to trim the edges of the pan. Lay a parchment paper on the dough cups, pour on some baking beans and bake in the oven until golden brown, 15 to 20 minutes.

Remove the pans from the oven, pour out the baking beans, and allow cooling.

In a medium bowl, mix the cashew cream, date sugar, and vanilla extract.

Divide the mixture into the tart cups and top with berries. Serve immediately.

Nutritional info per serving

Calories 545 | Fats 33.5g| Carbs 53.6g | Protein 10.6g

Mixed Nut Chocolate Fudge

Preparation Time: 2 hours 10 minutes

Servings: 4

A recipe for chocolate fudge that takes just 10 minutes to make and requires ingredients that are readily available.

Ingredients

3 cups unsweetened chocolate chips

¼ cup thick coconut milk

1 ½ tsp vanilla extract

A pinch salt

1 cup chopped mixed nuts

Directions

Line a 9-inch square pan with baking paper and set aside.

Melt the chocolate chips, coconut milk, and vanilla in a medium pot over low heat.

Mix in the salt and nuts until well distributed and pour the mixture into the square pan.

Refrigerate for at least for at least 2 hours.

Remove from the fridge, cut into squares and serve.

Nutritional info per serving

Calories 907 | Fats 31.5g| Carbs 152.1g | Protein 7.7g

Date Cake Slices

Preparation Time: 1 hour 20 minutes

Servings: 4

With a slightly thick yet fluffy texture, they're super soft.

Ingredients

½ cup cold plant butter, cut in pieces, plus extra for greasing

1 tbsp flax seed powder + 3 tbsp water

½ cup whole-wheat flour, plus extra for dusting

¼ cup chopped pecans and walnuts

1 tsp baking powder

1 tsp baking soda

1 tsp cinnamon powder

1 tsp salt

1/3 cup water

1/3 cup pitted dates, chopped

½ cup pure date sugar

1 tsp vanilla extract

¼ cup pure date syrup for drizzling.

Directions

Preheat the oven to 350 F and lightly grease a round baking dish with some plant butter.

In a small bowl, mix the flax seed powder with water and allow thickening for 5 minutes to make the flax egg.

In a food processor, add the flour, nuts, baking powder, baking soda, cinnamon powder, and salt. Blend until well combined.

Add the water, dates, date sugar, and vanilla. Process until smooth with tiny pieces of dates evident.

Pour the batter into the baking dish and bake in the oven for 1 hour and 10 minutes or until a toothpick inserted comes out clean. Remove the dish from the oven, invert the cake onto a serving platter to cool, drizzle with the date syrup, slice, and serve.

Nutritional info per serving

Calories 850 | Fats 61.2g| Carbs 65.7g | Protein 12.8g

Chocolate Mousse Cake

Preparation Time: 40 minutes + 6 hours 30 minutes chilling

Servings: 4

Have a cake with a basic mousse of chocolate and tell me how you feel.

Ingredients

2/3 cup toasted almond flour

¼ cup unsalted plant butter, melted

2 cups unsweetened chocolate bars, broken into pieces

2 ½ cups coconut cream

Fresh raspberries or strawberries for topping

Directions

Lightly grease a 9-inch springform pan with some plant butter and set aside.

Mix the almond flour and plant butter in a medium bowl and pour the mixture into the springform pan. Use the spoon to spread and press the mixture into the bottom of the pan. Place in the refrigerator to firm for 30 minutes.

Meanwhile, pour the chocolate in a safe microwave bowl and melt for 1 minute stirring every 30 seconds.

Remove from the microwave and mix in the coconut cream and maple syrup.

Remove the cake pan from the oven, pour the chocolate mixture on top making to sure to shake the pan and even the layer. Chill further for 4 to 6 hours.

Take out the pan from the fridge, release the cake and garnish with the raspberries or strawberries.

Slice and serve.

Nutritional info per serving

Calories 608 | Fats 60.5g| Carbs 19.8g | Protein 6.3g

Apricot Tarte Tatin

Preparation Time: 30 minutes + 1 hour chilling

Servings: 4

The fruit variety is the best overall, but it also goes well with apricots – happiness on a table.

Ingredients

For the piecrust:

4 tbsp flax seed powder + 12 tbsp water

¼ cup almond flour + extra for dusting

3 tbsp whole-wheat flour

½ tsp salt

¼ cup plant butter, cold and crumbled

3 tbsp pure maple syrup

1 ½ tsp vanilla extract

For the filling:

4 tbsp melted plant butter + more for brushing

3 tsp pure maple syrup

1 tsp vanilla extract

1 lemon, juiced

12 apricots, halved and pitted

½ cup coconut cream

3 to 4 fresh basil leaves to garnish

Directions

Preheat the oven to 350 F and grease a large pie pan with cooking spray.

In a medium bowl, mix the flax seed powder with water and allow thickening for 5 minutes.

In a large bowl, combine the flours and salt. Add the plant butter and using an electric hand mixer, whisk until crumbly. Pour in the flax egg, maple syrup, vanilla, and mix until smooth dough forms. Flatten the dough on a flat surface, cover with plastic wrap, and refrigerate for 1 hour.

After, lightly dust a working surface with almond flour, remove the dough onto the surface, and using a rolling pin, flatten the dough into a 1-inch diameter circle. Set aside.

In a large bowl, mix the plant butter, maple syrup, vanilla, and lemon juice. Add the apricots to the mixture and coat well.

Arrange the apricots (open side down) in the pie pan and lay the dough on top. Press to fit and cut off the dough hanging on the edges. Brush the top with more plant butter and bake in the oven for 35 to 40 minutes or until golden brown, and puffed up.

Remove the pie pan from the oven, allow cooling for 5 minutes, and run a butter knife around the edges of the pastry. Invert the dessert onto a large plate, spread the coconut cream on top, and garnish with the basil leaves. Slice and serve.

Nutritional info per serving

Calories 484 | Fats 33.8g| Carbs 46.4g | Protein 2.8g

Chocolate & Pistachio Popsicles

Preparation Time: 5 minutes + 3 hours chilling

Servings: 4

A popsicle is one of those wonders full of endless possibilities that are creative and mouth-watering.

Ingredients

½ cup unsweetened chocolate chips, melted

1 ½ cups oat milk

1 tbsp unsweetened cocoa powder

3 tbsp pure date syrup

1 tsp vanilla extract

A handful pistachios, chopped

Directions

In a blender, add chocolate, oat milk, cocoa powder, date syrup, vanilla, pistachios, and process until smooth. Divide the mixture into popsicle molds and freeze for 3 hours.

Dip the popsicle molds in warm water to loosen the popsicles and pull out the popsicles.

Nutritional info per serving

Calories 315 | Fats 17.8g| Carbs 34.9g | Protein 11.9g

Strawberry Cupcakes With Cashew Cheese Frosting

Preparation Time: 35 minutes + 30 minutes chilling

Servings: 4

To make this lovely pink ganache, you just need three basic ingredients. With freshly strawberry puree, it takes on a buttery flavor.

Ingredients

For the cupcakes:

2 cups whole-wheat flour

¼ cup cornstarch

2 ½ tsp baking powder

1 ½ cups pure date sugar

½ tsp salt

¾ cup unsalted plant butter, room temperature

3 tsp vanilla extract

1 cup strawberries, pureed

1 cup oat milk, room temperature

For the frosting:

¾ cup cashew cream

2 tbsp coconut oil, melted

3 tbsp pure maple syrup

1 tsp vanilla extract

1 tsp freshly squeezed lemon juice

¼ tsp salt

2-4 tbsp water as needed for blending

Directions

Preheat the oven to 350 F and line a 12-holed muffin tray with cupcake liners. Set aside.

In a large bowl, mix the flour, cornstarch, baking powder, date sugar, and salt.

Using an electric mixer, whisk in the plant butter, vanilla extract, strawberries, and oat milk until well combined.

Divide the mixture into the muffin cups two-thirds way up and bake in the oven for 20 to 25 minutes or until golden brown on top and a toothpick inserted comes out clean. Remove the cupcakes and allow cooling while you make the frosting.

In a blender, add the cashew cream, coconut oil, maple syrup, vanilla, lemon juice, and salt. Process until smooth. If the mixture is too thick, add some water to lighten the consistency a little. Pour the frosting into medium and chill for 30 minutes.

Transfer the mixture into a piping bag and swirl mounds of the frosting onto the cupcakes. Serve immediately.

Nutritional info per serving

Calories 853 | Fats 42g| Carbs 112.8g | Protein 14.3g

Nut Stuffed Sweet Apples

Preparation Time: 35 minutes

Servings: 4

This nut Stuffed Baked Apples are a buzz-friendly sliding dessert, or say, one or two weekend desserts snack.

Ingredients

4 gala apples

3 tbsp pure maple syrup

4 tbsp almond flour

6 tbsp pure date sugar

6 tbsp plant butter, cold and cubed

1 cup chopped mixed nuts

Directions

Preheat the oven the 400 F.

Slice off the top of the apples and use a melon baller or spoon to scoop out the cores of the apples. In a bowl, mix the maple syrup, almond flour, date sugar, butter, and nuts.

Spoon the mixture into the apples and then bake in the oven for 25 minutes or until the nuts are golden brown on top and the apples soft. Remove the apples from the oven, allow cooling, and serve.

Nutritional info per serving

Calories 581 | Fats 43.6g| Carbs 52.1g | Protein 3.6g

Classic Pecan Pie

Preparation Time: 50 minutes + 1 hour chilling

Servings: 4

The traditional pie is baked to a lustrous brown pecan load.

Ingredients

For the piecrust:

4 tbsp flax seed powder + 12 tbsp water

1/3 cup whole-wheat flour + more for dusting

½ tsp salt

¼ cup plant butter, cold and crumbled

3 tbsp pure malt syrup

1 ½ tsp vanilla extract

For the filling:

3 tbsp flax seed powder + 9 tbsp water

2 cups toasted pecans, coarsely chopped

1 cup light corn syrup

½ cup pure date sugar

1 tbsp pure pomegranate molasses

4 tbsp plant butter, melted

½ tsp salt

2 tsp vanilla extract

Directions

Preheat the oven to 350 F and grease a large pie pan with cooking spray.

In a medium bowl, mix the flax seed powder with water and allow thickening for 5 minutes. Do this for the filling's flax egg too in a separate bowl.

In a large bowl, combine the flour and salt. Add the plant butter and using an electric hand mixer, whisk until crumbly. Pour in the crust's flax egg, maple syrup, vanilla, and mix until smooth dough forms.

Flatten the dough on a flat surface, cover with plastic wrap, and refrigerate for 1 hour.

After, lightly dust a working surface with flour, remove the dough onto the surface, and using a rolling pin, flatten the dough into a 1-inch diameter circle.

Lay the dough on the pie pan and press to fit the shape of the pan. Use a knife to trim the edges of the pan. Lay a parchment paper on the dough, pour on some baking beans and bake in the oven until golden brown, 15 to 20 minutes. Remove the pan from the oven, pour out the baking beans, and allow cooling.

In a large bowl, mix the filling's flax egg, pecans, corn syrup, date sugar, pomegranate molasses, plant butter, salt, and vanilla. Pour and spread the mixture on the piecrust. Bake further for 20 minutes or until the filling sets. Remove from the oven, decorate with more pecans, slice, and cool. Slice and serve.

Nutritional info per serving

Calories 992 | Fats 59.8g| Carbs 117.6 g | Protein 8g

Summer Banana Pudding

Preparation Time: 25 minutes + 1 hour

Servings: 4

It's a no bake dessert that's perfect for a group's last minute get together. Just that something that everyone loves!

Ingredients

1 cup unsweetened almond milk

2 cups cashew cream

¾ cup + 1 tbsp pure date sugar

¼ tsp salt

3 tbsp cornstarch

2 tbsb cold plant butter, cut into 4 pieces

1 tsp vanilla extract

2 medium banana, peeled and sliced

Directions

In a medium pot, mix the almond milk, cashew cream, date sugar, and salt. Cook over medium heat until slightly thickened, 10 to 15 minutes.

Stir in the cornstarch, plant butter, vanilla extract, and banana extract. Cook further for 1 to 2 minutes or until the pudding thickens. Dish the pudding into 4 serving bowls and chill in the refrigerator for at least 1 hour. To serve, top with the bananas and enjoy!

Nutritional info per serving

Calories 466 | Fats 29.9g| Carbs 47.8g | Protein 4.3g

Cranberry Truffles

Preparation Time: 15 minutes

Servings: 4

Of sweet little cranberry pops, these cranberry truffles are creamy. They're a tasty little surprise and they make a really cute present.

Ingredients

2 cups fresh cranberries

2 tbsp pure date syrup

1 tsp vanilla extract

16 oz cashew cream

4 tbsp plant butter

3 tbsp unsweetened cocoa powder

2 tbsp pure date sugar

Directions

Set a silicone egg tray aside.

Puree the cranberries, date syrup, and vanilla in a blender until smooth.

Add the cashew cream and plant butter to a medium pot. Heat over medium heat until the mixture is well combined. Turn the heat off.

Mix in the cranberry mixture and divide the mixture into the muffin holes. Refrigerate for 40 minutes or until firm.

Remove the tray and pop out the truffles.

Meanwhile, mix the cocoa powder and date sugar on a plate. Roll the truffles in the mixture until well dusted and serve.

Nutritional info per serving

Calories 882 | Fats 66.35g| Carbs 64.5g | Protein 19.95g

Mango & Lemon Cheesecake

Preparation Time: 20 minutes + 3 hours 30 minutes chilling Servings: 4

This No Bake Mango Cheesecake is a love treat perfect and delicious!

Ingredients

2/3 cup toasted rolled oats

¼ cup plant butter, melted

3 tbsp pure date sugar

6 oz cashew cream cheese

¼ cup coconut milk

1 lemon, zested and lemon juiced

¼ cup just-boiled water

3 tsp agar agar powder

1 large ripe mangoes, peeled and chopped

Directions

Process the oats, butter, and date sugar in a blender until smooth.

Pour the mixture into a greased 9-inch springform pan and press the mixture onto the bottom of the pan. Refrigerate for 30 minutes until firm while you make the filling.

In a large bowl, using an electric mixer, whisk the cashew cream cheese until smooth.

Beat in the coconut milk, lemon zest, and lemon juice.

Mix the boiled water and agar agar powder until dissolved and whisk this mixture into the creamy mix. Fold in the mangoes.

Remove the cake pan from the fridge and pour in the mango mixture. Shake the pan to ensure a smooth layering on top. Refrigerate further for at least 3 hours.

Remove the cheesecake from the fridge, release the cake pan, slice, and serve.

Nutritional info per serving

Calories 337 | Fats 28g| Carbs 21.3g | Protein 5.4g

Plum Cashew Cheesecake

Preparation Time: 20 minutes + 3 hours 30 minutes chilling Servings: 4

Cheesecake is the favorite of most people and combined with cashew and plum, excellency is bestowed on us.

Ingredients

2/3 cup toasted rolled oats

¼ cup plant butter, melted

3 tbsp pure date sugar

6 oz cashew cream cheese

¼ cup oats milk

¼ cup just-boiled water

3 tsp agar agar powder

4 plums, cored and finely diced

2 tbsp toasted cashew nuts, chopped

Directions

Process the oats, butter, and date sugar in a blender until smooth.

Pour the mixture into a greased 9-inch springform pan and press the mixture onto the bottom of the pan. Refrigerate for 30 minutes until firm while you make the filling.

In a large bowl, using an electric mixer, whisk the cashew cream cheese until smooth. Beat in the oats milk.

Mix the boiled water and agar agar powder until dissolved and whisk this mixture into the creamy mix. Fold in the plums.

Remove the cake pan from the fridge and pour in the plum mixture. Shake the pan to ensure a smooth layering on top. Refrigerate further for at least 3 hours.

Take out the cake pan, release the cake, and garnish with the cashew nuts.

Slice and serve.

Nutritional info per serving

Calories 354 | Fats 26.7g| Carbs 27.7g | Protein 6.4g

Matcha Cheesecake

Preparation Time: 20 minutes + 3 hours 30 minutes chilling Servings: 4

This is a soft and simple cheesecake with green tea powder included to give it an extra yummy taste!

Ingredients

2/3 cup toasted rolled oats

¼ cup plant butter, melted

3 tbsp pure date sugar

6 oz cashew cream cheese

¼ cup almond milk

1 tbsp matcha powder

¼ cup just-boiled water

3 tsp agar agar powder

2 tbsp toasted hazelnuts, chopped

Directions

Process the oats, butter, and date sugar in a blender until smooth.

Pour the mixture into a greased 9-inch springform pan and press the mixture onto the bottom of the pan. Refrigerate for 30 minutes until firm while you make the filling.

In a large bowl, using an electric mixer, whisk the cashew cream cheese until smooth. Beat in the almond milk and mix in the matcha powder until smooth.

Mix the boiled water and agar agar until dissolved and whisk this mixture into the creamy mix. Fold in the hazelnuts until well distributed.

Remove the cake pan from the fridge and pour in the cream mixture. Shake the pan to ensure a smooth layering on top. Refrigerate further for at least 3 hours.

Take out the cake pan, release the cake, slice, and serve.

Nutritional info per serving

Calories 650 | Fats 59.33g| Carbs 25.84g | Protein 13.54g

Brown Butter Pumpkin Pie

Preparation Time: 1 hour 10 minutes + 1 hour chilling

Servings: 4

Give it a try when you want to use your own fresh pumpkin or squash.

Ingredients

For the piecrust:

4 tbsp flax seed powder + 12 tbsp water

1/3 cup whole-wheat flour

½ tsp salt

¼ cup plant butter, cold and crumbled

3 tbsp pure malt syrup

1 ½ tsp vanilla extract

For the filling:

2 tbsp flax seed powder + 6 tbsp water

4 tbsp plant butter

¼ cup pure maple syrup

¼ cup pure date sugar

1 tsp cinnamon powder

½ tsp ginger powder

1/8 tsp cloves powder

¼ tsp salt

1 (15 oz) can pumpkin purée

1 cup almond milk

Directions

Preheat the oven to 350 F. In a bowl, mix flax seed powder with water and allow thickening for 5 minutes. Do this for the filling's flax egg too in a separate bowl. In a bowl, combine the and salt. Add in plant butter and whisk until crumbly. Pour in the crust's flax egg, maple syrup, vanilla, and mix until smooth dough forms. Flatten the dough on a flat surface, cover with plastic wrap, and refrigerate for 1 hour.

After, lightly dust a working surface with flour, remove the dough onto the surface, and using a rolling pin, flatten the dough into a 1-inch diameter circle. Lay the dough on a greased pie pan and press to fit the shape of the pan. Use a knife to trim the edges of the pan. Lay a parchment paper on the dough, pour on some baking beans and bake for 15-20 minutes. Remove, pour out the baking beans, and allow cooling.

In a bowl, whisk filling's flax seed, butter, maple syrup, date sugar, cinnamon powder, ginger powder, cloves powder, salt, pumpkin puree, and almond milk. Pour the mixture onto the piecrust and bake further for 35-40 minutes. Slice and serve afterwards.

Nutritional info per serving

Calories 544 | Fats 31g| Carbs 58.4g | Protein 9.8g

How To Calculate Protein RDA Best For Your Body

Healthy protein is a vital nutrient; its intake is essential for the wellness of your muscle mass and, for the wellness of the heart. Consuming healthy protein can, also, aid you handle specific illness and sustain your weight-loss initiatives. The quantity of healthy protein you need to take in is based upon your weight, exercise, age and various other variables.

The RDA For Protein

The Recommended Dietary Allowance, or RDA, for healthy protein is based on your weight. Most individuals ought to take in 0.8 grams of healthy protein per kilo of body weight. Aspects such as whether you are a professional athlete or are an expectant woman can additionally play an important factor in your healthy protein consumption.

Individuals can eat up to 2 grams of healthy protein per kilo of bodyweight without long-term consequences. According to a 2016 evaluation post in the Journal of Food Functionality, the bearable limitation of healthy protein intake is 3.5 grams per kilo of body weight: it is basically more than 4 times than the basic amount that the RDA suggests for healthy protein. Extreme healthy protein consumption over a long-term period might impact the gastrointestinal, kidneys or vascular wellness.

Computing The RDA For Protein

To figure out just how much healthy protein you ought to be consuming, there is a simple formula: take your weight, which you most likely recognize in extra pounds, and then you need to transform it to kgs. The ordinary American male evaluates to have 195.7 extra pounds (matching approximately 88.77 kilos), while the typical American woman evaluates to have 168.5 extra pounds (which amounts to a concerning 75.21 kilos).

Considering that most individuals need to consume about 0.8 grams of healthy protein per kilo of body weight, this implies that the RDA formula is:

- (0.8 grams of healthy protein) x (weight in kilos).

Provided this standard, many males should consider that they should have an intake of 71 grams of healthy protein daily, due to the fact that 0.8 x 88.77 = 71.016. Ladies should eat around 60 grams of healthy protein each day, considering that the equation gives 0.8 x 75.21 = 60.168.

You can additionally simply increase your weight in extra pounds by 0.36 grams of healthy protein if you are having problem computing your body weight in kilos. This would change the RDA formula to the following:

- (0.36 grams of healthy protein) x (weight in extra pounds).

There is a selection of healthy protein consumption calculators offered online if you are not comfortable in computing your RDA for healthy protein by hand. You can use sites like the "United States Department of Agriculture's Dietary Reference Intakes Calculator".

Individuals Who Need More Protein

The RDA for healthy protein usually is 0.8 gram per kilo of body weight, lots of individuals can take in extra healthy protein safely. Professional athletes, for example, can eat as much of healthy protein as they desire as they burn a lot by exercising. Other individuals, like expecting females, nursing mothers and older generations additionally require eating even more of this nutrient.

The quantity of healthy protein you ought to eat as a professional athlete relies on the sort of exercise you take part in. Generally, individuals carrying out different workout routines ought to eat:

- Minimum exercise (periodic stroll or extending): 1.0 gram of healthy protein per kilo of body weight.

- Modest exercise (regular weight-lifting, quick strolling): 1.3 grams of healthy protein per kg of body weight.

- Extreme training (professional athletes, routine joggers): 1.6 grams of healthy protein per kilo of body weight.

Expectant ladies, likewise, require eating even more healthy protein than the standard suggested. According to a 2016 research in the Journal of Advances in Nutrition, women need to take in between 1.2 and 1.52 grams of healthy protein per kilo of weight every day while pregnant.

The reduced quantity (1.2 grams) is appropriate for very early maternities stages of around 16 weeks, while the top quantity is advised for later maternities of about 36 weeks. The assumption of healthy protein by expectant ladies isn't just crucial for the development of the fetus; it is additionally vital in assisting the mothers' body prepare to nurse their kids.

How To Calculate Your Protein Needs

It is crucial that we consume a sufficient amount of healthy protein each day to cover our body's requirements. Do you recognize just how much healthy protein you require? Numerous professional athletes and other people that work out a lot assume that they ought to enhance their healthy protein consumption to assist them to shed their weight or construct even more muscle mass. It is real that the extra you work out, the higher your healthy protein requirement will undoubtedly be.

Healthy Protein Intake Guidelines

Healthy proteins are the standard foundation of the body. They are comprised of amino acids and are required for the formation of muscular tissues, blood, skin, hair, nails, and the wellbeing of the interior body's organs. Besides water, healthy protein is one of the most abundant compounds in the body, and the majority of it is in the skeletal muscle mass.

Considering this, it is assuring to understand that according to the Dietary Guidelines for Americans between 2015-2020, most individuals obtain sufficient healthy protein daily. The very same record directs out that the consumption of fish and shellfish, and plant-based proteins such as seeds and nuts, are frequently lacking.

If you are an athlete, nonetheless, your healthy protein requirements might be somewhat greater considering that resistance training and endurance exercises can swiftly break down muscular tissue healthy protein.

The basic standards for strength-trained and endurance professional athletes, according to the Academy of Nutrition and Dietetics, Dietitians of Canada, and the American College of Sports Medicine, is the recommended amount laying in between 1.2 and 2 grams of healthy protein per kg of body weight to achieve maximum efficiency and the health and wellness of the body.

If you are attempting to gain even more muscular tissue, you might assume that you require a lot more healthy protein, yet this isn't what you should do. There is proof that very strict professional athletes or exercisers might take in even more healthy protein (over 3 grams/kilograms daily), but for the typical exerciser, consumption of as much as 2 grams/per kg daily suffices for building muscle mass.

Various Ways To Determine Protein Needs

When establishing your healthy protein requirements, you can either recognize a percent of overall day-to-day calories, or you can target in detail the number of grams of healthy protein to eat each day.

Percent of daily calories

Present USDA nutritional standards recommend that adult males and females should take an amount in between 10 and 35 percent of their overall calories intake from healthy protein. To obtain your number and to track your consumption, you'll require to understand the number of calories you eat daily.

To keep a healthy and balanced weight, you need to take in about the same variety of calories that you burn daily.

Just increase that number by 10 percent and by 35 percent to obtain your variety when you understand precisely how many calories you take in daily.

As an example, a male that eats 2,000 calories each day would more or less require to eat between 200 to 700 calories every day of healthy protein.

Healthy protein grams each day

As an option to the portion method, you can target the specific amount of healthy protein grams each day.

One straightforward method to obtain an amount of healthy protein grams daily is to equate the percent array into a particular healthy protein gram variety. The mathematical formula for this is very easy.

Each gram of healthy protein consists of 4 calories, so you will just need to split both calorie array numbers by 4.

A guy that consumes 2,000 calories daily must take in between 200 and 700 calories from healthy protein or 50 to 175 grams of healthy protein.

There are various other methods to obtain a much more specific number which might consider lean muscular tissue mass and/or exercise degree.

You can establish your fundamental healthy protein requirement as a percent of your complete day-to-day calorie consumption or as a series of healthy protein grams daily.

Healthy protein needs based on weight and activity

The ordinary adult demands a minimum of 0.8 grams of healthy protein per kg of body weight each day. One kg equates to 2.2 extra pounds, so an individual that has 165 extra pounds or 75 kg would more or less require around 60 grams of healthy protein daily.

Your healthy protein requirements might raise if you are very active. The Academy of Nutrition and Dietetics, American College of Sports Medicine and the Dietitians of Canada, recommend that professional athletes require even more healthy protein.

They recommend that endurance professional athletes (those that often take part in sports like running, biking, or swimming) take in 1.2 to 1.4 grams of healthy protein per kilo of body weight daily which equates to 0.5 to 0.6 grams of healthy protein per extra pound of body weight.

The companies recommend that strength-trained professional athletes (that engage in exercises like powerlifting or weightlifting often) take in 1.6 to 1.7 grams of healthy protein per kg of body weight. This equates to 0.7 to 0.8 grams of healthy protein per extra pound of body weight.

Healthy protein needs based on lean body mass

A new approach of finding out how much healthy protein you require is focused on the degree of the exercise (how much energy you spend) and your lean body mass. Some professionals really feel that this is an exact extra method because our lean body mass needs extra healthy protein for upkeep than fat.

Lean body mass (LBM) is merely the quantity of bodyweight that is not fat. There are various methods to identify your lean body mass, yet the most convenient is to deduct your body fat from your overall body mass.

You'll require to establish your body fat percent. There are various methods to obtain the number of your body fat consisting of screening with skin calipers, BIA ranges, or DEXA scans. You can approximate your body fat with the following calculating formula.

To determine your overall body fat in extra pounds, you will need to increase your body weight by the body fat portion. If you evaluate yourself to be 150 pounds and that your fat percent is 30, then 45 of those bodyweight pounds would certainly be fat (150 x 30% = 45).

Compute lean body mass. Merely deduct your body fat weight from your overall body weight. Utilizing the exact same instance, the lean body mass would certainly be 105 (150 - 45 = 105).

Calculating Your Protein Needs

While the above standards offer you a general idea of where your healthy protein consumption needs to drop, determining the quantity of day-to-day healthy protein that's right for you, there is another method that can assist you in tweaking the previous results.

To identify your healthy protein requirements in grams (g), you need to initially determine your weight in kgs (kg) by separating your weight in pounds by 2.2.

Next off, choose the number of grams of healthy protein per kilo of bodyweight that is appropriate for you.

Use the reduced end of the array (0.8 g per kg) if you consider yourself to be healthy but not very active.

You should intake a more significant amount of protein (in between 1.2 and 2.0) if you are under tension, expecting, recuperating from a health problem, or if you are associated with extreme and constant weight or endurance training.

(You might require the recommendations of a physician or nutritional expert to assist you to establish this number).

Increase your weight in kg times the number of healthy protein grams per day.

For instance:

A 154 pound man that has as a routine exercising and lifting weights, but is not training at an elite degree:

154 lb/2.2 = 70 kg.

70 kg x 1.7 = 119 grams healthy protein each day.

Healthy protein as a percent of complete calories

An additional means to determine how much healthy protein you require is utilizing your everyday calorie consumption and the percentage of calories that will certainly originate from healthy protein.

Figure out exactly how many calories your body requires each day to keep your current weight.

Discover what your basic metabolic rate (BMR) is by utilizing a BMR calculator (often described as a basic power expense, or BEE, calculator).

Figure out the amount of calories you burn via day-to-day tasks and include that number to your BMR.

Next off, choose what portion of your diet plan will certainly originate from healthy protein. The percent you pick will certainly be based upon your objectives, physical fitness degree, age, type of body, and your metabolic rate. The Dietary Guidelines for Americans 2015-2020 advises that healthy protein represent something in between 10 percent and 35 percent for grownups suggested caloric intake.

Multiply that percentage by the complete variety of calories your body requires for the day to establish overall everyday calories from healthy protein.

Split that number by 4. (Quick Reference - 4 calories = 1 gram of healthy protein.)

For instance:

A 140-pound woman that eats 1800 calories each day consuming a diet plan having 20 percent of the total caloric intake consisting of healthy protein:

1800 x 0.20 = 360 calories from healthy protein.

360 calories/ 4 = 90 grams of healthy protein each day.

Compute daily protein need

To establish your day-to-day healthy protein requirement, increase your LBM by the suitable task degree.

- Less active (normally non-active): increase by 0.5.
- Light task (consists of strolling or horticulture): increase by 0.6.
- Modest (30 mins of a modest task, thrice weekly): increase by 0.7.
- Energetic (one hr of workout, 5 times regular): increase by 0.8.
- Really energetic (10 to 20 hrs of regular workout): increase by 0.9.
- Professional athlete (over 20 hrs of regular workout): increase by 1.0.

Based upon this approach, a 150-pound individual with an LBM of 105 would certainly need a day-to-day healthy protein amount that varies between 53 grams (if inactive) to 120 grams (if very active).

How Many Grams Of Protein Should You Eat Per Kilogram Of Body Weight?

The quantity of healthy protein you take in is essential for your wellness. Lots of people ought to take in 0.8 grams of healthy protein per kilo of body weight, however, this quantity can alter based upon different elements. Individuals that are expecting, lactating, that have particular health and wellness problems or that are extremely energetic, commonly need even more healthy protein than the standard.

Healthy protein requirement per kilogram

You need to recognize your healthy protein demand per kg of body weight. Basically, the Recommended Dietary Allowance or RDA for healthy protein is 0.8 gram per kg of body weight.

Specific diet plans, like low-carbohydrate diet plans or the Atkins diet and even paleo diet regimens, might need you to eat even more healthy protein than this while still permitting you to take in a well-balanced diet regimen. Various other diet plans, like the Dukan diet or the predator diet regimen, concentrate on consuming only healthy protein and fat.

Raising the quantity of healthy protein you consume can be healthy and balanced and excellent, mainly if the healthy protein you are eating is originating from different resources. However, according to the Harvard Medical School, taking in even more than 2 grams of healthy protein per kg of body weight or even more can be harmful to your wellness.

According to the Centers for Disease Control, the ordinary American male values 195.7 extra pounds (or 88.77 kilos), while the typical American lady values 168.5 extra pounds (or 75.21 kilos). Given that the RDA is 0.8 grams of healthy protein for every single kilo of body weight, this indicates that a lot of males need to take in about 71 grams of healthy protein daily. Females that are a bit smaller sized ought to generally take in around 60 grams of healthy protein each day.

Plant-Based Diets Myths

You Can Not Obtain Enough Healthy Protein On A Plant-Based Diet

You cannot get enough healthy protein on a plant-based diet... that's what many people think when they think about going vegan. "Where will I get my protein?" or "Do I require to combine foods to get appropriate protein?"

The Recommended Daily Allowance (RDA) for healthy protein for most individuals is 0.8 grams of healthy protein per kilo of healthy and balanced body weight. This is attainable while complying with a plant-based diet regimen. There is a multitude of plant foods that are rich sources of healthy protein. These consist of:

• Tofu.

• Lentils.

• Beans.

• Nuts.

• Seeds.

• Entire grains.

Also, people that require more healthy protein, such as very active adults, elders, and children, can effectively enhance their consumption by eating these foods.

The American Dietetic Association concurs that well-planned diets that exclude or limit animal products are nutritionally appropriate and healthier compared to those that do not. Also, plant-based diet regimens are connected with lower rates of cardiovascular disease, high blood pressure, cancer cells, and kind 2 diabetic issues.

Lastly, healthy protein from a selection of plant foods specifical starches like rice, beans, and corn, eaten throughout a day, appear to have of all vital amino acids. Inevitably, you should consume plants to your heart's desire, and keep in mind the simple understanding that you're getting ample protein if your calorie needs are being satisfied.

Plant-Based Diet Regimens Are Limiting

When I first started a plant-based diet regimen, I had no idea about what I had to eat what I could eat. Looking back, it's clear that my diet regimen had been so fixated on chicken, dairy, and highly refined foods that what I required was a change in viewpoint.

Meats can be switched with mushrooms, tofu, and beans in meals. Date-sweetened treats - as opposed to sugar or syrup-based treats - are scrumptious and plentiful.

A research study demonstrates, however, that boosts in muscle mass and toughness is connected with protein no matter of the resource.

You'll Be Hungry On A Plant-Based Diet Regimen

Usually, buddies or clients set many appointments concerning the switching over to a plant-based diet plan, based on the worry of being hungry. It subjectively seems as though they can't be pleased because plants are low in calorie density. Nonetheless, as fruits, veggies, whole grains, and vegetables are all high in fiber - which is most likely to leave you feeling fuller for longer - this shouldn't be an issue.

A plant-based diet regimen does not supply adequate vitamins and minerals

This myth could not be further from the truth. Plants are, without a doubt, one of the most nutrient-dense foods we can eat. Leafy greens and beans are rich in zinc, iron, and calcium, and berries are extremely high in vitamin K and manganese, and also tropical fruits like mangoes and pineapples are high in vitamin C. Ultimately, the more diverse your diet is, the better - not to discuss, broadening your taste experience is amazing for your taste buds.

That stated, plant-based eaters must supplement with vitamin B-12, as this vitamin comes from the soil. This is the only vitamin you can't get on a plant-based diet regimen.

In spite of the typical myths, following a plant-based diet can supply you with appropriate macronutrients, and doesn't need to be boring or cost you your entire salary. So, if you're still considering a plant-based diet, it's time to draw up a grocery store listing, prepare in your recipes and begin the food preparation!

10 Tips for Success on the Plant-Based Diet

If you take an objective look at the Mediterranean diet, you have to admit that for the most part, this does not sound very difficult to follow. Nonetheless, transitioning to any new diet is something that takes work and dedication, and it can be helpful to have some advice along the way. In the following, we offer some tips for success on the Mediterranean diet.

1. Use fruit for dessert

As we learned, when looking at the Mediterranean diet pyramid, consuming sweets is something that should only be done on special occasions. However, a lot of us need something sweet to top off a good meal. A good way to continue enjoying dessert without putting your health at risk is to substitute some fruit for the usual dessert items like cake and ice cream. Make a bowl of strawberries, raspberries, and blueberries instead. You can top it off with a small amount of low-fat whipped cream or even drizzle your fruit with some honey if you have a real sweet tooth. Also, consider adding small amounts of dark chocolate.

2. Use Home-made Salad Dressing

Believe it or not, salad dressing can be a problematic food item. The reason is that salad dressings made by large companies often contain unhealthy oils like soybean oil that should be avoided on a Mediterranean diet. They may also contain excessive amounts of sugar and processed chemicals. You can make your own simple yet very tasty salad dressings at home, so you know exactly what you are getting. Naturally, the number one ingredient in any homemade salad dressing should be extra virgin olive oil.

3. Snack on Nuts and Seeds

Nuts and seeds form an important part of the Mediterranean diet, and we all get in-between meal hunger pangs from time to time. Try satisfying them with a handful of nuts or seeds instead of the usual things you tend to snack on. This will help you get more healthy monounsaturated fat along with some good dietary fiber. People who make no changes to their diet other than increasing the amount of nuts and seeds consumed have been shown to have significantly lower heart disease risk. Regular consumption of nuts and seeds also lowers the level of inflammation in the body.

4. Enjoy Red Wine with Meals

The consumption of red wine is something that is often pointed out when discussing the Mediterranean diet, and we've talked about it a lot in this book. The best way to consume red wine is with your meals Daily consumption of red wine is fine as long as you are not drinking to excess or drinking outside of your meals. You probably don't want to drink on an empty stomach, and consumption should be in moderation. That means 1-2 drinks per day for women and 1-3 drinks per day for men.

5. Make Sure You're Getting Genuine Olive Oil

A few years back, the New York Times ran a shocking news story. It turns out that a lot of the olive oil on the market is fake. In many cases, cheap oils that are actually unhealthy, like canola oil, are dyed to make them look like olive oil. Even more shocking, many of the fake olive oils come from Italy and Greece. The best way to avoid this problem is to look up which olive oils are known to be genuine. The University of California, Davis, for example, has a lab that tests olive oil brands to find out if they are the real deal or not. One brand that has been confirmed to be genuine is California Olive Ranch. There is also an olive oil association, and you can check their lists to determine if the brands that you see in the store are genuine olive oils. Remember that if you are getting a fake or diluted olive oil, you might not be getting the full health benefits that you think you are getting, and could even be doing yourself some harm. Also look for extra virgin olive oil that is packed in green bottles, since this is necessary to protect the oil from damage that could be caused by full exposure to outside light.

6. Eat Avocados

The avocado originally came from the region that is called Mexico today, so it's not a part of the traditional Mediterranean diet. But of course, neither is salmon. But like salmon, avocado is a mix and match food that can be included on a Mediterranean diet, because it contains the same types of fats that olive oil does. Avocados are also excellent sources of dietary fiber, potassium, and magnesium, and they even give you some vitamin C. They can also help to make your meals more filling when you are consuming low-fat protein items.

7. Spice it Up

Good spices are a crucial part of the Mediterranean diet. You can help make your dishes more appealing by adding the right mix of spices. Do a little research to see what kinds of spices are used in dishes throughout the Mediterranean basin, and mix it up. Try going Portuguese one night, and Middle Eastern on another night. Variety, as they say, is the spice of life.

8. Try a Meatless Day

Meat in moderation is a key component of the Mediterranean diet, and one easy way to accomplish this goal is to have a day without eating meat at all. Consider using chickpeas as your protein source in some of your meals, rather than consuming meat. The humble chickpea has a great flavor and makes a wonderful addition to any dish. It's been used since ancient Roman times, and in fact, the first pizza crusts in ancient Rome were actually made out of a flour that was made entirely from chickpeas. Other types of beans and legumes can be used to supply your protein needs on meatless days.

9. Eat Slowly and Eat Socially

We mentioned the idea of trying to eat in social situations when possible. Another big difference between the cultures of the Mediterranean basin and the cultures of America and northern Europe is that the Mediterranean way of eating is not a rushed affair. In the Mediterranean, people like to eat slowly and take their time with their meals. This helps make eating more enjoyable and helps with digestion. Americans, especially, tend to want to eat as quickly as possible. Consider taking a different approach and see how it feels.

10. Plan Ahead

Once you get into the swing of things and the foods that you should be eating on the Mediterranean diet become a habit, making your meals will be a snap. But in the beginning, you might find yourself sitting around wondering what you should eat. Get ahead of the curve by planning out your meals in advance while in the first few months of the diet. That way you won't get yourself in a bind, where you either have nothing to eat or aren't sure what to eat, and you get tempted to make a fast-food run.

Meal Plan

Day	Breakfast	Lunch	Dinner	Smoothie
1	Mexican-Spiced Tofu Scramble	Teriyaki Tofu Stir-fry	Mushroom Steak	Chocolate Smoothie
2	Whole Grain Protein Bowl	Red Lentil and Quinoa Fritters	Spicy Grilled Tofu Steak	Chocolate Mint Smoothie
3	Healthy Breakfast Bowl	Green Pea Fritters	Piquillo Salsa Verde Steak	Cinnamon Roll Smoothie
4	Healthy Breakfast Bowl	Breaded Tofu Steaks	Butternut Squash Steak	Coconut Smoothie
5	Root Vegetable Hash With Avocado Crème	Chickpea and Edamame Salad	Cauliflower Steak Kicking Corn	Maca Almond Smoothie
6	Chocolate Strawberry Almond Protein Smoothie	Thai Tofu and Quinoa Bowls	Pistachio Watermelon Steak	Blueberry Smoothie
7	Banana Bread Breakfast Muffins	Black Bean and Bulgur Chili	BBQ Ribs	Nutty Protein Shake
8	Stracciatella Muffins	Cauliflower Steaks	Spicy Veggie Steaks With veggies	Cinnamon Pear Smoothie
9	Cardamom Persimmon Scones With Maple-Persimmon	Avocado and Hummus Sandwich	Mushroom Steak	Vanilla Milkshake

	Cream			
10	Activated Buckwheat & Coconut Porridge With Blueberry Sauce	Chickpea Spinach Salad	Spicy Grilled Tofu Steak	Raspberry Protein Shake
11	Sweet Molasses Brown Bread	Teriyaki Tofu Stir-fry	Piquillo Salsa Verde Steak	Raspberry Almond Smoothie
12	Mexican-Spiced Tofu Scramble	Red Lentil and Quinoa Fritters	Butternut Squash Steak	Chocolate Smoothie
13	Whole Grain Protein Bowl	Green Pea Fritters	Cauliflower Steak Kicking Corn	Chocolate Mint Smoothie
14	Healthy Breakfast Bowl	Breaded Tofu Steaks	Pistachio Watermelon Steak	Cinnamon Roll Smoothie
15	Healthy Breakfast Bowl	Chickpea and Edamame Salad	BBQ Ribs	Coconut Smoothie
16	Root Vegetable Hash With Avocado Crème	Thai Tofu and Quinoa Bowls	Spicy Veggie Steaks With veggies	Maca Almond Smoothie
17	Chocolate Strawberry Almond Protein Smoothie	Black Bean and Bulgur Chili	Mushroom Steak	Blueberry Smoothie
18	Banana Bread Breakfast	Cauliflower Steaks	Spicy Grilled Tofu Steak	Nutty Protein Shake

	Muffins			
19	Stracciatella Muffins	Avocado and Hummus Sandwich	Piquillo Salsa Verde Steak	Cinnamon Pear Smoothie
20	Cardamom Persimmon Scones With Maple-Persimmon Cream	Chickpea Spinach Salad	Butternut Squash Steak	Vanilla Milkshake
21	Activated Buckwheat & Coconut Porridge With Blueberry Sauce	Teriyaki Tofu Stir-fry	Cauliflower Steak Kicking Corn	Raspberry Protein Shake
22	Sweet Molasses Brown Bread	Red Lentil and Quinoa Fritters	Pistachio Watermelon Steak	Raspberry Almond Smoothie
23	Mexican-Spiced Tofu Scramble	Green Pea Fritters	BBQ Ribs	Chocolate Smoothie
24	Whole Grain Protein Bowl	Breaded Tofu Steaks	Spicy Veggie Steaks With veggies	Chocolate Mint Smoothie
25	Healthy Breakfast Bowl	Chickpea and Edamame Salad	Mushroom Steak	Cinnamon Roll Smoothie
26	Healthy Breakfast Bowl	Thai Tofu and Quinoa Bowls	Spicy Grilled Tofu Steak	Coconut Smoothie
27	Root Vegetable	Black Bean and	Piquillo Salsa	Maca Almond

	Hash With Avocado Crème	Bulgur Chili	Verde Steak	Smoothie
28	Chocolate Strawberry Almond Protein Smoothie	Cauliflower Steaks	Butternut Squash Steak	Blueberry Smoothie

Conclusion

Moving to vegan bodybuilding diet is a great idea as it will pump in the requisite amounts of protein and also keep up the energy levels that are a must for someone doing hard-core workouts. Remember to take enough of macronutrients into the system and in the right form. Include the above-recommended protein sources into your diet and feel the protein levels rising by a considerable. It will require patience, hard work, and dedication to stick to a vegan meal plan, but in the long-run, it will surely payout.

Perhaps a plant-based diet can be a high-protein diet when consumed with the right approach and understanding. Such awareness is important for people building their muscles or those who are involved in athletic activities. They are the ones who need protein the most for the strengthening of their muscles. In this cookbook, we have not only tackle the plant-based diet, but it is written with the sole purpose of providing a high-protein diet to vegan bodybuilders and athletes. There are several plant-based sources that can be coupled with some plant-based supplements to meet the daily protein needs of a person. Give it a good read and try all of its high-protein plant-based recipes. Break all the myths of veganism by maintaining a rock-solid body and healthy body shape.

To help you further is a vegan bodybuilding cookbook that has some innovative and some conventional recipes using plant-based protein sources to give your vegan diet a push. Try out these exciting recipes using a variety of protein sources into the diet plan and watch your protein intake blossom. They are a fine mix of soups, salads, and main course dishes, infusing the richness of multiple spices, vegetables, fruits, nuts, and oils. The wide variety of recipes found in the vegan bodybuilding cookbook is specially made, keeping in mind the requirements of bodybuilders. So eat healthy to stay healthy!

Printed in Poland
by Amazon Fulfillment
Poland Sp. z o.o., Wrocław

64805969R00074